Trophies
of
Heaven

Trophies of Heaven

BY RON KNOTT

TROPHIES OF HEAVEN

By Ron Knott

©1985, Ron Knott

Assigned to Word Aflame Press, 1986
Reprint History: 1990, 1991, 1992, 1995, 1999, 2000, 2001, 2002

Cover Design by Tim Agnew

Printed in United States of America

Printed by

WORD AFLAME®PRESS
8855 DUNN ROAD
HAZELWOOD, MO 63042-2299

Library of Congress Cataloging-in-Publication Data

Knott, Ron

    Trophies of Heaven.

    1. Witness bearing (Christianity) I. Title.
BV4520.K62 1986   248'.5   86-26649
ISBN 0-932581-06-4

Thanks for the teaching and leadership from my pastors: John Benson, Jack DeHart, Jerry Green, O. C. Marler and all the other fine ministers of the United Pentecostal Church.

Sincerely

Ron Knott

CONTENTS

Part II

FOREWORD

The chapters in this book are from the heart of a burdened soulwinner. They contain the basic methods of witnessing this glorious truth of the Spirit-filled apostolic movement. They tell of the miracles, the healings, transformation of lives. You will see the diverse operation of the Spirit leading a soulwinner to hungry souls.

As you read this book the excitement will grip your heart. You will be challenged and convinced by the methods shown here that everyone can be a soulwinner.

Ron Knott represents in the kingdom all that he has written of here. He is a layman that has blessed thousands of people, here and abroad, by the continual giving of his time, talents, finances, and keen insight of methods. He is a man that is used of God.

Ron is a very successful businessman, with holdings in real estate, gas and oil, and a Mercedes-Benz dealership. He is employed by Delta airlines as a pilot with rank of Captain.

Beyond all that God has blessed Ron with, you will see a man that is humble, teachable, loyal to the local church, eager to help others, ready and willing at any time to be involved in the Kingdom's work.

God bless you as you read this refreshing book.

J. C. Benson, Pastor
Euless, Texas

INTRODUCTION

What is on your schedule one hundred years from today? Could I make an appointment with you 100 years from tonight? Let's have a party in your suite June 14, 99 years from today. Does your calendar or appointment book extend out that far? These are some questions I have asked people that are not saved. You would be surprised how those questions get their attention. They stop, blink their eyes, shuffle their feet and squirm around for an answer. You can tell the question digs deep into their thoughts. Most will come back with the reply, "Well, I really haven't thought that far ahead."

This is the condition of most people of this world. They only live for today and the immediate future and blank out any thought of the long term. I then tell them we all are on a journey whether we realize it or not. We are traveling at the rate of 60 seconds per minute, 60 minutes per hour, 24 hours per day, 7 days per week, 30 days per month and 365 days per year. We are heading toward that 100-year appointment at the above speed. Then I ask them, "Where will you be when that appointed time arrives?" Again they squirm around without an answer, or some might say, "I plan to get right with the Lord someday." I point out the fact that a lot of people plan on becoming eleventh hour Christians but they die at 10:30. It's our responsibility to get them before they pass into eternity.

My reason for writing this book is to bring to the attention of our brothers and sisters that there are many people we can reach if only we will witness to them. I have included several methods and examples here as a guide.

11

Develop your own style and your own method and practice, practice, practice. Granted we will not win everyone, but if we only win one soul that is worth more than all the world.

God did not call us to be judges or lawyers, but He has subpoenaed all of us as witnesses. Peter denied Christ three times by not acknowledging Him. How many times have we denied Him in the crowds of this world by not saying we know Him? Therefore be quick to talk to God about your friends, relatives and neighbors, and be quick to talk to your friends, relatives and neighbors about God.

Daniel Webster was once asked, "Mr. Webster, what is the most sobering, searching thought that ever entered your mind?" Without hesitancy he replied, "My personal accountability to God!"

PART I

chapter one

TROPHIES OF HEAVEN

Have you ever noticed how hunters and fishermen display their trophies, kills, or catches they have accomplished? How eager they are to tell you just how they stalked that big deer or caught the big fish mounted on the wall of their home or office? This is their pride and joy. They enjoy showing all their trophies and reminding themselves of their great feats.

Many offices I have visited have all four walls decorated with the big fish with weight and date of the catch engraved in brass for all to see. Others brag about the 8 or 10 point buck that didn't get away. They are quick to tell just exactly how long it took. How they had to get up before daylight and get on the stand to wait out the prize kill. Many will tell you it took years of hunting before they got the one they were after.

The hunter went to much expense and traveled many miles just to get the opportunity to hunt. He bought the best equipment he could find and spent hours reading about the nature of the game in order to know the animal's habit patterns. He waited with great expectation until the season opened or until the trip could be made. Many times he planned just how he was going to make the final move that would assure him a successful hunt. Perhaps you have done the same. I know I have.

Why can't we work as hard to win a soul? Why can't we be as proud of that eternal trophy that we have won or will win? The woods are full of them. There is no shortage, no endangered species. Season is open. Now is the time "to bag the trophy."

This trophy is one that you can be proud of throughout all eternity. In fact, Jesus has a special reward for the ones who are soul hunters. There is a special crown for this kind of Christian. These are the only trophies that you can take from this earth to heaven. They will be there waiting for you when you arrive.

It might be an embarrassing day when you arrive in heaven and are asked about your trophies. What excuse will you have then? I don't think any will be sufficient. Do you?

Just think how proud you can be when your report shows 10 on your account, or 20, or 100, or more. You can have as many as you want. There is no limit. There are no restrictions as far as size, shape, color, age, or sex. Each soul is a tremendous trophy in the sight of God.

One of the reasons for this book is to help others know that they too can be soulwinners. You can have a wall full of trophies when you get to heaven. The streets of gold will be nice, gates of pearl very unusual, but soulwinning is accomplished by the Lord working with us. Only mankind can win a soul. The saints who have died and are in the presence of God cannot win a soul. Only we who are alive and have the truth plus the desire can achieve the great task.

Yes, my fellow Christians, if we spent as much time planning our search for the lost soul as we do on other hunting trips we might be more productive. If we tithe our time as we do our money, we would be more productive for Christ. As an example there are 720 hours in one month. Do you give God 72 hours of that month? We go to church two hours Sunday morning, two hours Sunday night, and two hours Wednesday night. That's six hours a week or twenty-four hours a month. What do you do with the next 48 hours that you owe God? Perhaps I can help you find more time to share Jesus with your neighbors.

You know as well as I that not everyone will be won to the Lord. Nor can you catch *all* the fish, or kill *all* the deer, but if you are persistent you will win some.

A few days ago a friend of mine told me how he killed his first deer. He said, "My brother-in-law told me to get up before daylight, go climb up in this big tree near the deer run, and just sit and wait. Well, I did that. I sat up in that tree all day long. I was cold, hungry and very uncomfortable but no deer came by. So I went back and told my brother-in-law that I had wasted the whole day and had not seen one deer."

The brother-in-law told him to go back the second morning and repeat the same procedure as the day before. Again he was cold, hungry, and uncomfortable the second day and still no deer came by. He said to himself, "I'll not do this again. There are no deer in these parts." The brother-in-law convinced him to go just one more morning.

On the third day when he had about given up all hope

17

of even seeing a deer, this big buck stopped right under the tree where he was sitting. The kill was easy and the trophy is shown to all that come by his home.

You have to be persistent: then God will send that hungry soul your way when you least expect it. Also you must be ready, willing, and able to deliver the "Word that is sharper than any two-edged sword."

I have read stories of men going west to pan for gold during the gold rush. They would pan for hours and days dipping up the rocks and mire trying to find just one small nugget among all the trash. They kept on and on until they hit pay dirt and came up with the nugget they were after. One soul is worth more than all the gold!

"He who goes out weeping, carrying seed to sow, will return with songs of joy, carrying sheaves with him" (Psalm 126:6, NIV).

chapter two

SHEEP BEGET SHEEP

This chapter attempts to compile facts on the subject of witnessing. I used to think it was the pastor's responsibility to do all the witnessing to the lost souls in his area. But the fact is, shepherds don't beget sheep; sheep beget sheep. Therefore, it is our responsibility as laymen to do the witnessing.

Laymen cannot pay pastors to do their soulwinning anymore than they can pay pastors to get their own souls to heaven. The pastor of a church should no more be expected to win all the souls within his community than is the captain of a company of infantrymen expected to do all the fighting in a battle. The captain is expected to do some fighting, some expert fighting, but his greatest responsibility is to direct the soldiers in a battle.

"The pastor is also like an automobile dealer who maintains a group of salesmen in his force. He does not do all the selling himself. He does sell some cars to certain customers, but he does it by way of demonstration, instruction, and leadership for his salesmen."

This was written by Reverend Leavell in the early 1900s and is still true today.

One of the first prayers that I prayed when the Lord so graciously filled me with the Holy Ghost was, "Lord, give me the ability to tell others about this great gift." My actual prayer was "Lord, give me wisdom and knowledge of your Word and courage enough to tell my fellowman about this great plan of salvation."

That's one prayer that the Lord is ready and willing to answer for anyone. If you don't believe it, just try Him. I have asked the Lord to let me witness to someone knowing that I was completely safe because no one was going to be around for me to witness to but before the day was over, God would arrange for a hungry soul who wanted to hear about the truth of God's Word to come my way either in person or by phone. I'll give some examples later.

When I first came into the church I was shocked at the lack of material on how to witness. Moreover, I was surprised that most people didn't know how to effectively tell about this great gift that Jesus had bled and died for. But even worse is the fact that a lot of so-called Christians don't want to be bothered with witnessing. "That's for the preacher to do, or Brother So and So's responsibility, or I am not cut out to be a witness," they would say. Let's see what the Scriptures say about our responsibility to God on this subject.

"Ye shall be witnesses unto me both in Jerusalem, and in all Judea, and in Samaria, and unto the uttermost part of the earth" (Acts 1:8).

Let's change this Scripture to apply to today: "Ye shall

be witnesses unto me both in Dallas, and in all of Texas, and the United States, and unto the uttermost part of the earth." Just add the name of your town and state to this Scripture and that's your responsibility.

> *"Son of man, I have made thee a watchman . . . give them warning from me. When I say unto the wicked, Thou shalt surely die; and thou givest him not warning, . . . to save his life; the same wicked man shall die in his iniquity; but his blood will I require at thine hand" (Ezekiel 3:17-18).*
>
> *"If the watchman see the sword come, and blow not the trumpet, and the people be not warned; if the sword come, and take any person from among them, he is taken away in his iniquity; but his blood will I require at the watchman's hand" (Ezekiel 33:6).*
>
> *"For unto whomsoever much is given, of him shall be much required" (Luke 12:48).*
>
> *"Even so faith, if it hath not works, is dead, being alone" (James 2:17).*

There are many other Scriptures that teach us to witness.

Why is there a need to witness? Let me ask you this question. How did you come to the truth? Did you one day drop or kick open the Bible and it flipped to Acts 2:38, or did you hear a loud voice from heaven saying, "Obey Acts 2:38," or did you have an angel from heaven whisper in your ear, "Repent and be baptized everyone of you in the name of Jesus Christ for the remission of sins and ye shall receive the gift of the Holy Ghost," or did the truth get to you as it did in the examples in the Bible? That is, someone explained the Word of God to you. The Lord sent a man to talk to the eunuch in Acts the eighth chapter. The eunuch was reading the Bible and was asked by Philip, "Understandest thou what thou readest?" His answer in the thirty-first verse was, "How can I, except some man should guide me?"

Another example is in the tenth and eleventh chapters of Acts with Cornelius. First, let's look at Cornelius's credentials. He was a devout man and one who feared God with all his house, which gave much alms to the people, and prayed to God always. This sincere man would put most of us to shame. But he was sincerely wrong. How did God get him on the right path to heaven? Well, God just happened to have nearby a good witness named Peter. God knew He could depend upon Peter so He disturbed him with a dream. God also saw the sincere heart of Cornelius and gave him a vision. Why did the Lord go to all the trouble to arrange this meeting? No other reason than to get the saving words to this man, Cornelius, who was doing all he knew to obey God, yet he had fallen short.

So the Lord uses men to spread the truth. That's the reason He says, "Ye shall be witnesses." God could have used angels but He chose to give us (mankind) the opportunity. Man is given the responsibility, honor, and privilege of presenting the most precious gift ever given to mankind.

This is a better deal than the hottest tip in the stock market, or the inside knowledge of a great oil and gas discovery, or the discovery of the lost gold mine. This gift is worth more than all the riches in the whole world according to the Bible. So why be ashamed to go tell somebody? We should be more excited about this gift than we would be if we just learned that we had somehow received one billion dollars! Could you keep that fact quiet, or would everyone around you know of your great gain? The same should be true of this gift of salvation. Everyone around you should know how great it is. Would you share it with them? If not they may never know.

My own testimony is not much different from others. I had accepted Jesus Christ as my personal Savior, yet that action on my part only made me hungrier for more truth. I even went to another church and asked for the Holy Ghost and the Lord gave me that precious gift, yet I still knew something was missing. So after attending five different organizations, I asked the Lord to please give me the truth and please give me the truth today. I was very confused up to this point because I saw people doing mighty works in the name of Jesus, even prophesying in His name, yet iniquity was great among them. (See Matthew 7:21-23.) I saw many healings, tongues and interpretations of tongues, yet I knew something was lacking. That Sunday afternoon when I asked God for the truth He knew that I was sincere. Thank God He answered my prayer that very day.

No, I didn't hear a loud voice from heaven, nor did an angel appear unto me, but a *man* whom God could trust called me that night and said, "The Lord impressed me to call you concerning your salvation." I had never attended his church, he was in a city several hundred miles away, yet the Lord heard my cry and sent the answer by *man*.

That's why there is a need to witness. It's God's way of spreading this great truth. Therefore one of the greatest responsibilities and privileges of a Christian is to be ready, willing, and able to respond to the need of presenting the truth to a lost soul when God so directs you.

Individual witnessing is God's method to win the lost. God's method is men. He could have used angels or principalities but God gave us not only the command but the opportunity to work for Him.

Have you ever considered the power that you have backing up your effort when you are sharing God's Word? We have all of heaven behind us. Don't underestimate the power of God's Word.

> *"So shall my word be that goeth forth out of my mouth: it shall not return unto me void, but it shall accomplish that which I please, and it shall prosper in the thing whereto I sent it"* (Isaiah 55:11).

Look at Luke:

> *"I say unto you, that likewise joy shall be in heaven over one sinner that repenteth, more than over ninety and nine just persons, which need no repentance . . . Likewise, I say unto you, there is joy in the presence of the angels of God over one sinner that repenteth"* (Luke 15:7, 10).

Can't you just see the scene in heaven when you lead one lost soul to repentance? The grandstands of heaven are looking down on the earth in excitement over one sinner coming to repentance. This is much greater than any earthly touchdown or homerun that we view from the bleachers. These are angels of God the Scripture says, yet this act of repentance is so important to the angels that it adds joy in their presence.

Want to add a little joy in heaven in the presence of God? All we have to do is lead one to repentance, and as busy as the angels are carrying out the duties of God, they stop and observe this one. Why do you think that it is so important to them? Because their God and Master died that this sinner might be saved. Look at Acts:

> *"Take heed therefore unto yourselves, and to all the flock over the which the Holy Ghost hath made you overseers, to feed the church of God, which he hath purchased with his own blood"* *(Acts 20:28).*

Do you honestly believe that men are lost? Peter said in Acts:

> *"For there is none other name under heaven given among men, whereby we must be saved"* *(Acts 4:12).*

If Christians believe what Christians profess to believe, that is, that there is a heaven to which men may be saved, and that there is a hell to which the unsaved will be damned, then they should have love enough for their fellowman to witness to them about the rewards at each place. Jesus said:

> *"Except ye repent, ye shall all likewise perish"* *(Luke 13:5).*

25

That's why Jesus said, "Go out into the highways and hedges, and compel them to come in" (Luke 14:23).

What is the price of one soul? No one but God can put a value on a soul. We do know that He said that if a man gains the whole world and loses his soul he has lost all. So we know that a man's soul is worth more than all the gold, silver, oil, gas, land, and fame that this world can offer.

Therefore, the next time you meet one of these creatures called man coming down the street, or in the restaurant, or in your place of business, think about that soul whom the Lord has packaged in the flesh. Yes, that soul will live forever. It will be in a place of rest and peace or in a place of torment that burneth with fire forever and ever.

Only you have the key to the knowledge that will save that person. If we keep this knowledge of God's Word locked up in our hearts then we are of all men most selfish. The Bible says:

> *"Eye hath not seen, nor ear heard, neither have entered into the heart of man, the things which God hath prepared for them that love him"* (I Corinthians 2:9).

The Lord died that all might have eternal life. If He only wanted us to be saved then He should have had us killed moments after we received the Holy Ghost, so that we would be with Him immediately in heaven. No, He said, "He that received seed into the good ground is he that heareth the word, and understandeth it: which bringeth forth, some an hundredfold, some sixty, some thirty" (Matthew 13:23).

26

Jesus said, "When I come I will bring my reward with me." Now I know that He must have a very good accounting system. For we are told that everything we do and everything we say is recorded. So the Lord must have a big pencil (thank goodness it has a big eraser on one end because He wiped away my sins with it). The Lord knows how much, or how little you do for His kingdom.

I knew a man that owned 1/32 interest in an oil well. This 1/32 interest paid him over one million dollars per month. Think about it! How would you like the royalties on 1/32 of a soul? You might well be the 32nd person who asked that soul to come to church or perhaps you prayed with him around the altar. Yet God knows what part you played and He will reward you for the effort. Think what you might have if you gave him a Home Bible Study, prayed, and fasted for him.

I doubt that there will be many souls won by only one person, but we are a team, each doing what the Lord leads us to do in order to win that soul, and you will be given credit for your part no matter how large or small it is.

We often think what's the use, there is no way that we can win the world. There is an overwhelmingly greater number in the world than in the church, so we are fighting a hopeless battle. We give up before we start.

That's a trick of the devil. He likes for you to fail and draw back into your corner ashamed and defeated.

The world population is approximately 4.2 billion people. As an example, suppose you really wanted to be a great witness and you had the ability to organize 500 different people a day to tell about Jesus Christ. If you did accomplish this great task of assembling 500 different people a day, it would take 24,658 years for you to teach the gospel one time to every person in the world. Of course, you would not take a vacation or day off during this period and the world would experience no population growth during these 24,658 years! As you can see by this example there is no way that the world could be won.

Let's suppose that you only witness to one soul who demonstrates a willingness to know, love, and glorify Jesus. After this one is won you work with him in order that he might be brought to maturity. You spend time with him in all types of situations. You teach him how to study the Bible and to pray. You teach him church doctrine and other facts. You teach him to witness for Jesus then send him out to witness himself. Then he wins one soul and instructs and teaches his candidates to win others. The geometric progression of soulwinning would look like this table below. We have thought too big—world evangelism starts at our front door—one on one:

1st year	you +	1 =	2 souls
2nd year	2 +	2 =	4 souls
3rd year	4 +	4 =	8 souls
4th year	8 +	8 =	16 souls
5th year	16 +	16 =	32 souls
6th year	32 +	32 =	64 souls
7th year	64 +	64 =	128 souls
8th year	128 +	128 =	256 souls
9th year	256 +	256 =	512 souls
10th year	512 +	512 =	1,024 souls
11th year	1,024 +	1,024 =	2,048 souls
12th year	2,048 +	2,048 =	4,096 souls
13th year	4,096 +	4,096 =	8,192 souls
14th year	8,192 +	8,192 =	16,384 souls

15th year	16,384 +	16,384 =	32,768 souls
16th year	32,768 +	32,768 =	65,536 souls
20th year		=	1,048,576 souls
32nd year		=	4,294,967,296 souls

(MORE THAN THE WORLD'S POPULATION!)

The above illustration is if you only win one soul a year and teach that person to win a soul then he teaches his candidate how to win a soul, and continue the process. In *32 short years*, not *24,658* years, the world could be won without the aid of television or other mass media means. The world could be won twice as fast if only two souls a year were won.

You might say this has been going on for years and look at the small number of church members we have. I believe the key here is for us to take time and teach, train, love, and feed the Word to the ones we win else they die. You know as well as I do that there are thousands who have been baptized in Jesus' name and have received the Holy Ghost, but are no longer in the church. Why? Could it be that we thought our task was complete when the work really begins? Recruiting is simple in comparison to training.

Taking that recruit and making a full-fledged warrior out of him makes him productive. If we stop with recruiting then our army will fail in the first battle because of a lack of proper training. Therefore spend time and teach your candidate the ways of the Lord. Teaching (discipling) others is the process by which a Christian with a life worth emulating commits himself for an extended period of time to a few individuals who have been won to Jesus, the purpose being to aid and guide their growth to maturity and equip them to reproduce.

Many people try to spread themselves thin and reach everyone in their community. The results of their efforts is that instead of reaching everyone, they reach no one. Their efforts would have been far more effective if they had just reached a few. Jesus said, "Do you truly love me? Feed my sheep." Again He said, "Do you truly love me? Feed my lambs" Jesus said, "Take care of my sheep" (John 21:16 *NIV*).

chapter three

GOD LOVES THE SINNER TOO!

Sometimes I am afraid that we as Christians limit God to our own church or group. We may not consider the fact that He loves that drunkard lying in the gutter as much as He loves us. Yes, God hates sin but loves the sinner.

Let us not get too far removed from the state of that sinner, wherever he is or whatever he is doing. Paul puts us in our place:

> *"Know ye not that the unrighteous shall not inherit the kingdom of God? Be not deceived: neither fornicators, nor idolators, nor adulterers, nor effeminate, nor abusers of themselves with mankind, nor thieves, nor covetous, nor drunkards, nor revilers, nor extortioners, shall inherit the kingdom of God. And such were some of you: but ye are washed, but ye are sanctified, but ye are justified in the name of the Lord Jesus, and by the Spirit of our God"* (I Corinthians 6:9-11).

31

And that is what some of us were. Therefore the *main* difference in the drunkard and the saint is that someone witnesses to that drunkard and he then becomes a saint as you and I did.

God is interested in our going to church, paying tithes, praying in the prayer room, singing, and teaching. He loves that kind of devotion. But let's take God out of church once in awhile and share Him with the world in order to win others.

Jesus was not crucified *in* a church, only *by* church leaders. He was killed at the kind of place where thieves curse and soldiers gamble. Because that is where He died, and since that is what He died about and who He died for, that is where Christians can share His message of love. That's what real Christianity is all about.

Jesus' ministry in our community is limited to us! Jesus died that His Spirit might take up abode in our bodies.

> *"What? know ye not that your body is the temple of the Holy Ghost which is in you, which ye have of God, and ye are not your own?"* (I Corinthians 6:19).

His abode is not in buildings made of wood and stone but within us. Therefore we have to take Him out of the church into the world where the sinners are. You and I are His body.

> *"For we are members of his body, of his flesh, and of his bones"* (Ephesians 5:30).

Jesus must witness through the church, His body, not the congregation or our denomination. But, through you and me.

Look at the early church. In just two years they made the Word of the Lord heard by all they that dwelt in Asia. (See Acts 19:10). How did they accomplish such? They had no church building. They visited every home in the city of Ephesus and all in Asia minor.

> *"So mightily grew the word of God and prevailed" (Acts 19:20).*

These people had 20-20 vision. Look at Acts 20:20-21: "But have shewed you, and have taught you publickly, and from house to house, testifying both to the Jews, and also to the Greeks."

This was the start of the *Home Bible Study* program. They might not have called it *Search For Truth* or *Exploring God's Word,* but it served the same purpose. It works as well today as it did then, 2000 years ago!

Did it work? Read Acts 19:10 again to see how completely it did work. How was it done? By personal soulwinning. Can you do it? Do you have the Holy Ghost?

> *"But ye shall receive power, after that the Holy Ghost is come upon you: and ye shall be witnesses unto me both in Jerusalem, and in all Judea, and in Samaria [in Texas, and Louisiana, and all the United States], and unto the uttermost part of the earth" (Acts 1:8).*

Where did Jesus witness to people? The Bible says in

the marketplace, on the streets, on the mountain sides, by the seashore, and in homes. He was criticized by religious leaders for doing so.

> *"This man receiveth sinners, and eateth with them" (Luke 15:2).*

He commanded us to go out into the highways and hedges, and compel them to come in, that His house may be filled. (See Luke 14:23). He said in John:

> *"For this cause came I into the world, that I should bear witness unto the truth" (John 18:37).*

Jesus never said go sit in the church building and wait for them to come in. He said go out and get them. The Bible says:

> *"And daily in the temple, and in every house, they ceased not to teach and preach Jesus Christ" (Acts 5:42).*

Ordinarily we have church three times a week. Have you ever thought about the fact that the bars and dance halls, liquor stores, and other sinful places are open every day? Is it asking too much for us to take Jesus with us every day and tell others about Him? The church is a place to learn more about the doctrines of Jesus and to be nourished in His Word. It's not a very good place to catch a sinner. When you try to catch a fish you normally go where the fish are. When you try to catch a sinner you have to go where he is. I don't mean to go into the dens of sin such as bars and dance halls, but go to his home, to his work, to his everyday activities. This was the method the early church used.

"The harvest truly is plenteous, but the labourers are few" (Matthew 9:37).

The last thing that Jesus commanded us to do was:

"Go ye into all the world, and preach the gospel to every creature" (Mark 16:15).

You don't have to be a missionary or a clergyman to be a soulwinner. You simply must want to obey God's Word.

I am afraid many nice church-going people may be court-martialed for not going and witnessing as our Captain (Jesus) has commanded us to do. Paul said:

"Woe is unto me, if I preach not the gospel!" (I Corinthians 9:16).
"Let your light so shine before men, that they may see your good works, and glorify your Father which is in heaven" (Matthew 5:16).

Have you ever heard the above Scripture quoted by people who would then say, "I don't believe we should go around talking about religion. I'll just let my light shine; then people will know where I stand."

Satan has used this very effectively to silence many Christians. What does the Bible say about this subject? Why is His Word called light?

> *"The entrance of thy words giveth light"*
> *(Psalm 119:130).*
> *"Thy word is a lamp unto my feet, and a light*
> *unto my path" (Psalm 119:105).*

The Word of God shines; God's Word is His light! What is your light? Let your light shine. What is your light? Your word! Therefore go tell somebody about Jesus. Jesus said:

> *"If I be lifted up from the earth, will draw all*
> *men unto me" (John 12:32).*

In summary, the Bible does not tell us to go into all the church but to go into all the world to witness for Him. We must put legs on our prayers and go to the sinners.

We must exercise physically in order to develop strength and stamina to endure hardness and testing. We must also exercise the plan of witnessing in order to develop ourselves as a witness. We learn by doing!

chapter four

YOU CAN DO IT!

One of the most common tricks of the devil is to convince you that you cannot witness. He can instill so much fear that we Christians crawl into our security blankets and hide any light that we might let shine into the lost world. He does this in many ways. The one that I want to address is the fear of failure.

The fear of failure comes in many varieties; such as, "I might say the wrong thing," or "This person really doesn't want to hear about this Pentecostal experience," or "Let someone else talk to him because I don't think he will listen to me." Many times we talk ourselves out of witnessing before we even get started. This surely makes old Satan happy. He wins the battle before it ever begins.

Think with me for a moment what is at stake when you use those excuses. (That's all they are—excuses.) An excuse is defined as a lullaby to soothe a guilty conscience. An eternal soul is at stake. It's up for grabs for the devil and his angels or the Lord and His angels. Whose army are you enlisted with? "Onward Christian Soldiers" should be our theme and we should go forward with all the fiery darts of truth and power that the Lord has given us to defeat the enemy. Don't be a coward or a turncoat. Don't lay your arms down without firing a shot. Go to the defense of that soul. That soul is in bondage just as though he were in a prisoner-of-war compound. The soul is not there of its own choosing. It has been defeated and captured by the enemy. Only we have the power to over-come the enemy with the Holy Ghost and free this soul from prison. We must act! We must not be afraid to act. If we don't act and act fast that soul will be lost.

Think of this as someone who stands by watching a blind man walking into a burning building unable to see the danger ahead and yet no one warns the blind man of his terrible destiny. If we believe the Bible, we are guilty of the same offense unless we warn the lost soul of its terri-ble destiny. So don't let the devil hinder you with all those negative thoughts.

I say that you have failed already if you don't take a stand. When you take a stand, then you have delivered your weapons. It's up to the Lord to guide your missiles of truth to the soft target of that soul. He knows just how to handle the situation. But you first must deliver the weapons of the Word. It has been said that the greatest thing about Christianity is Jesus Christ and the weakest thing about Christianity is Christians.

Let me ask you a personal question. What would the population of heaven be if all Christians were like you? Would the Lord have to increase His building program in order to have room for the extra ones or would there be a great depression in heaven? Well, we Christians are the only ones who can lead others to that wonderful place.

Think about it!

Every one of us is different in our approach to a given situation. The same is true in witnessing. You should develop your own style. Use the technique that you are most comfortable with. That way you can become more effective. We cannot choose whether or not we are going to set an example. The only choice we have is *what kind* of example we are going to set.

Never, never, never use the hard-nosed, belligerent tactics that, "You are wrong" and, "I am right" and, "If you don't do it my way you are going straight to hell." That's not a witness of Jesus Christ. Remember you are His ambassador, so act like one! He had love and compassion for the lost, not an arrogant attitude of, "I am better than you are."

The following is a list of points, which I review before, during, and after witnessing to a candidate. I call it my check list:

1) Did I make a favorable impression on him?
2) Did I talk from the candidate's viewpoint?
3) Did I find the strongest desire or need of the candidate and then capitalize on it?
4) Did I encourage the candidate to do part of the talking?
5) Did I give the candidate a reason for going to our church rather than elsewhere?
6) Did I properly convey the background and merits of Pentecost?
7) Did I use my Bible and tracts to the best advantage?
8) Did I overcome the candidate's objections without encouraging an argument?

9) Did I avoid letting the candidate get off the main subject?
10) Did I encourage the candidate to ask questions and did I answer them intelligently?
11) Did I make a proper summary of the main points of the plan of salvation?
12) Did I leave the door open for a successful call later?

THE SOULWINNER'S ALPHABET

Every Christian knows his ABC's and a quick run-down of the alphabet will show us that there is a corresponding characteristic for good witnessing in each letter:

Attitude – Always positive and cheerful, never belligerent.

Belief – Both in yourself and in God and in the message.

Challenge – To anticipate rather than fleeing.

Determination – The one quality that separates the true soulwinners from others.

Enthusiasm – About the Holy Ghost and our church.

Faith – In yourself and in God to give you power.

Goal – Set it, and let nothing stop you from achieving it; then set another one.

Humor – Always good but never overbearing.

Improve – Don't fall into the trap of complacency.

Joy – Demonstrate the joy of the Holy Ghost and make people want that joy.

Knowledge – Know more about the gospel by continuing to study the Word.

Listen – To your candidate. He may open a door and give you a clue to his needs.

Mature – The manner in which you should handle every phase of witnessing.

Notes – Make notes of the progress of your conversation with the person soon after you depart while they are fresh in mind. Review these notes before the next meeting.

Opportunity – Share it with others.

Progress – What you should achieve.

Quality – The extra ingredient that is helping you— namely the Holy Ghost.

Resistance – What you can overcome with perseverance and knowledge.

Service – Service to God, the candidate, the church, and yourself.

Telephone – To remind you that you have many lost friends who are just a phone call away.

Uniqueness – Nothing like what you have to offer.

Vitality – A happy, healthy mental and spiritual condition.

Work – What you need to do to become successful.

X – The "other brand" that you shouldn't belittle!

Yesterday – You can't change it. So try to do better today.

Zest – To put into your personality and presentation so that souls might be won.

chapter five

TOOLS OF THE TRADE

When I was a fighter pilot in the United States Navy, I had to know my aircraft and its related systems as well as I knew my own body. I had to know its capabilities and be able to get the maximum performance out of it in a moment's notice. These were life or death situations. The way I was able to know about this great machine was to read and study the handbook. The handbook had all the answers. It had normal operating procedures and emergency procedures.

I had to spend many hours studying to show myself approved before I was allowed to take off in this airplane which would go twice the speed of sound. I had to practice normal procedures so I could perform them without thinking. This is called overlearning. That is being able to react to a situation without having to think or having to open the book for an answer. Sometimes in an emergency situation you don't have time to think, just react.

Not only did I have to know my aircraft but I had to know the enemy's aircraft as well. I had to know his capabilities and performance envelopes. It was very important in a combat situation to know the enemy's capabilities in order to keep him from shooting me down. My aircraft was much superior to the enemy aircraft but if I did not use my weapons system properly then the enemy could come in with an inferior product and destroy me or what I stood for.

Don't you think we as Christians should know our handbook, the Holy Bible, so that when we go out to meet the enemy in a witnessing situation we won't get shot down by an inferior product? We should overlearn the Bible so that we will have instant recall on the verses of Scripture that are needed to defend our salvation. These are emergency procedures; it's a matter of life or death. We must react properly or a soul might be lost, just as an aircraft might be lost if we make the wrong turn in battle.

I had many weapons to fire at the enemy from my aircraft. I had guns, rockets, and bombs to destroy the works of the enemy.

We also have many weapons to destroy the devil and his army. We have the Bible, tracts, Home Bible Studies and others, but we must know how to properly use them to be most effective. We must overlearn our procedures. This can be easily accomplished by practice, practice, and practice.

Let me share with you the importance of knowing your handbook in all emergency situations. Recently a medical doctor in our area was praying and asking God if the Holy Spirit was for him. He just happened to come in contact with one of our laymen and this brother did a very good job of telling him what he ought to do. I was then contacted and asked to go visit with this doctor because he had more questions about this great gift. I called and made a luncheon appointment with him and was pleased to learn that he had set aside several hours for our discussion.

When I arrived at the doctor's office I introduced myself to this fine looking young doctor. He said, "Sir, I have a surprise for you."

I said, "Great, what is it?"

He said, "This meeting is so important to me because I really want to know the truth so I have invited my pastor to join in on the conversation." (His pastor was a member of a large southern denomination that teaches against the Holy Ghost and other important issues.)

This could have been a frightful experience for me had I not practiced, practiced, and practiced my procedures many times before. I had already overlearned the Scriptures and knew where the nuggets of truth were that would shoot down any half-truth doctrine.

After lunch the doctor asked the question, "What is the truth about salvation?" I let this well-educated minister tell his belief first. Then I began to let the Scriptures flow. I was not worried because truth was on my side. I had asked God early in my Christian experience to give me wisdom, knowledge and courage, enough to tell anyone about His beautiful plan.

After about one hour the minister had to agree with the Bible on who Jesus is, how to be baptized, and the fact that the Holy Spirit is for us today. He then left in a hurry. The doctor is a member of our church today and has won many others to this truth.

In a-situation like this I am reminded of Paul in Ephesians 6:13-14, 17, 19 *(NIV): "Put on the full armor of God so that when the day of evil comes, you may be able to stand your ground . . . Stand firm then, with the belt of truth buckled around your waist . . . Take the helmet of salvation and the sword of the Spirit which is the word of God . . . Pray also for me, that whenever I open my mouth, words may be given me so that I will fearlessly make known the mystery of the gospel."*

USING YOUR BIBLE

Let me share with you some hints on how to use your Bible effectively. Get a Bible that is easy for you to read. I suggest a New Testament that has subject titles throughout each chapter. This is very helpful when looking up different events. As you read your Bible, mark the areas that you want to come back to in a witnessing situation. You'll be surprised how easy it is to find a Scripture once you have marked it. You'll even know what part of the page it is on before you get back to the Scripture. Most Bibles have a few blank pages in the back. Use this space to write down important Scriptures. I have written in the back of my Bible John 5:43 which tells me the name of the Father, John 14:26 that tells me the name of the Holy Ghost, and Matthew 1:21 which tells me the name of the Son. If I forget them while talking to someone about baptism I will flip open that back page while they are not looking and ask them to read John 5:43. This builds their confidence in you because you are so skillful with the Scriptures. In most cases the people that you will be talking with know very little about the location of Scriptures in the Bible.

Another tool that I have found very useful is a small

46

notebook. It's about the same size as a small New Testament. I have all the Scriptures I can find on Eternal Security in one section, another section is on baptism, another is on the Holy Ghost, one on Mormons, another on faith and works, another on church history, one on the Godhead, and so forth. Every time I find another good Scripture on one of my subjects, I'll put it in my notebook. I can take that notebook and talk to any group about the plan of salvation. It took a little time to put it together but it's one of my best tools in witnessing. It's also good for review when I want to study. That little book is where I got a lot of my information for this book.

HOME BIBLE STUDIES

"Search for Truth" or "Exploring God's Word" are two very good Home Bible Study courses that you can teach with just a little practice. Both courses have a teacher's manual that is very easy to follow and covers the subject very well. These Home Bible Studies are without a doubt one of the best ways to lead people into the truth.

I have found that the Home Bible Study works best with just one couple at a time, preferably in their home. It's easy for them to forget about the lesson if it's in your home. If you are coming to their home, they will be there.

I have conducted many Home Bible Studies and as of this time I have never had one fail to win at least one out of the family. In most cases both will come into the church.

Many times I have had them come back and tell me how thankful they were that I spent time with them. The world is hungry for the truth. What is really beautiful to see is the ones with whom I have had Home Bible Studies are now giving the lessons to others. This is church growth.

The Home Bible Study gives the candidates an opportunity to ask questions, tell their belief, and also their needs. It is hard for them to ask questions in church. You can also have a Home Bible Study for persons who will not go to church—such as a husband or father. In most cases they will join in the conversation and study since it's being conducted in their own home.

Have your church order the small Home Bible Study kit for you. You can practice giving it to your own family until you feel proficient enough to tell others. Then ask your friends and neighbors to let you give them a free Home Bible Study. You will be surprised at the positive response that you will get. Most people are interested in their eternal destiny and will appreciate your offer.

I can't say enough about the Home Bible Study except it really does work. Try it, you'll like it. Not only are you doing something great for your neighbor and God but you will also increase your self-confidence, your witnessing ability, and your knowledge about the Bible.

MEN'S BIBLE STUDY

With my pastor's approval I recently started a men's Bible study at a local motel. The purpose of this meeting was to invite men that wouldn't come to church. We stressed that you bring your barber, baker, and banker. The results were surprising. Many were led to the full plan of salvation.

We met on the first Monday of each month. Coffee, cokes, and doughnuts were served for the first thirty minutes just to get acquainted. Then we would start with our planned program. The subject would be taken from any material in the Bible but always would lead around to the plan of salvation. We would start out by asking for prayer requests. Some of our men would ask prayer for the President of the United States and all other government officials. (See I Timothy 2:1-3.) Others would ask for special prayer for a sick friend or a loved one. We would all join hands and make an appeal for God to answer these requests. By this time the visitors could see that we were sincere and that we really had the ability to pray. This seemed to make them more relaxed and more interested in the program.

Next I would cover a short subject from the Bible that would easily lead into the plan of salvation. I would call on men to tell their experience of how they came into this beautiful truth. There would be many backgrounds represented there from our own fellow Christian brothers. Each told in his own way how God had revealed the truth to him. You could see the interest rising in the guests during each testimony. After this was over we asked if any one needed special prayer and one of our men would always have a need. He would ask us to gather around him, lay hands on him and pray for his need. It might be to help him to be a better witness or for a better job or some other need. Then we would extend the invitation to others. Many times a visitor that would not go to church or to an altar would ask us to pray for him. He would break down right then and there and began to pray himself. Many of these men were then easily led to the church.

49

We found out that men would express themselves more freely when not in the presence of women. When they saw successful businessmen praying, it was easier for them to pray. They didn't seem to have as much problem overcoming the macho image as they did in church. It worked!

One night someone brought a state highway patrolman to one of our meetings. This man sat back and observed us very carefully during the entire meeting. Just prior to the close he asked that we pray for him. He said that he had been raised by his grandmother who was a very devout Methodist, the old shouting kind. He said that he had a dream a few nights before about his grandmother who had gone on to be with the Lord. In the dream his grandmother came to him in a beautiful setting but was speaking in a language that he couldn't understand. He related to us, "Tonight when I heard you men speaking in tongues it was just like in my dream." He said, "I feel that God is telling me that I too must have this experience." We were delighted to hear that and began to explain the Word to him more fully. In a few days he was baptized in Jesus' name and filled with the Holy Ghost.

Another side effect of these meetings was that we found out more about our brothers in the church. They would ask us to pray for problems or situations that would never come up in the church. Of course our pastor was there in charge, yet on the sideline, so as not to make the visitor think we were teaming up on him through the minister.

The local cafeteria has a special meeting room for business meetings such as the Lions Club and Rotary Clubs. Occasionally we met in this room which is free of charge. We only paid for our food. This gave us an opportunity to invite men out to dinner giving us a chance to talk with them about the Bible after eating. Several were able to get their fellow-workers to come out to these meetings.

The men of the church really enjoyed the fellowship with each other in these meetings. We were able to learn more about our brothers and understand situations and conditions about each other that we were not aware of before. However, the main purpose was to lead other men to Jesus and this was accomplished.

THE POWER OF A TRACT

A friend of mine is a captain with Pan Am Airlines in Miami, Florida. I used to live in the same neighborhood with this pilot when I was also based in Miami. This pilot was one of the wildest playboys that I had ever known. I was not a church member of any kind while we were neighbors.

I moved from Miami to the Dallas/Ft. Worth area and was later filled with the Holy Ghost and baptized in Jesus' name.

Shortly after this great experience I called my friend in Miami to tell him about Jesus. I could hear him and his wife fussing and fighting while we were talking. Finally he told me in so many words that he thought I was off my rocker, and he was happy for me if I thought I was doing the right thing, but he didn't really have any interest in my new faith.

So what can you do for a fellow like that? Pray for him.

More than a year passed before I was in Miami again.

I called him just to see how they were doing. The first thing he asked was, "Ron, are you still hung up on that Jesus thing?"

"Yes, Sir! About 100%."

"Well, Praise the Lord, Brother."

I almost dropped the telephone. "What did you say?" Then he told me the following story.

"I was on a layover in Las Vegas, Nevada, a few weeks ago and the greatest experience happened to me, just like in the Bible," he said. "I was about to check out of my hotel room when I noticed I was thirty minutes too early for the scheduled pick-up time. There I was in full uniform with nothing to do for thirty minutes. So I felt in my uniform pocket and found this tract (he doesn't remember putting it in his pocket or where it came from). 'In order to amuse myself for thirty minutes I'll just stand before the mirror and read what is on this piece of paper like a great actor' I decided." Then he read down to a part that said to rebuke Satan in Jesus' name and he said, "For the life of me I couldn't say those words." He tried several times but couldn't say them.

The next thing he remembered was the phone ringing in his room. He looked at his watch and more than one hour had passed since he started to read that tract. He was lying across his bed. He said, "I was really afraid to answer the phone because I just knew it was flight operations calling wanting to know why I had missed pick-up." That's one thing that you don't do and keep your job. The company will lay you off in very short order for being late for a flight.

Finally he got up enough courage to answer the phone and sure enough it was flight operations calling him. But not for the reasons he thought. They told him, "Captain, we have been trying to call you for over an hour to inform you that your flight has been cancelled due to a tropical depression in the Miami area." The flight was to be delayed another twenty-four hours. What a relief, he thought.

He said, "Something strange is going on in this room." So he got out of his uniform and into civilian clothes and went downstairs and started to gamble. "I would take the wildest chances and still win." All the time something kept telling him to go back to the room and read that tract. He finally said, "God, if You are in this let me lose everything on the next roll." He lost then went back to his room to read the tract.

This time he read the tract in a prayerful manner. By the time he finished reading the tract he was speaking in a language he had never heard before. The Lord filled him with the Holy Ghost right then and there.

Then I had the opportunity to teach him about the Godhead and baptism. He, his wife, and two daughters are baptized in Jesus' name.

God loved that man so much that He caused a tropical depression many miles away in order to have a little time with my friend. That tract that someone had given him was the key to his salvation.

One of our great soulwinners in a church that I attended was won by a tract that he found in a washroom. This man was on dope, separated from his wife and in a desperate and lost condition. One of our church members placed that tract in the washroom. It had our church address and phone numbers stamped on the back. When this poor man found this ray of hope, he immediately called the church for help. The Lord soon filled him with His Spirit. His wife and children are all in the church and are doing a great work for the Lord.

Tracts are easy to carry and easy to give out. I leave them in hotel rooms inside the Gideon Bible. You can leave them for your waitress with your tip, place them in public restrooms, and mail them in your letters. Once I had to pay a lawyer attorney fees that was the result of a lawsuit that I thought was unfair. Every month I would put a tract in with my payment. Finally this lawyer called me and said that he really did enjoy reading the tracts and because of my concern for him that he was going to reduce the bill so I wouldn't have to make any more payments. I still don't know if he was really touched by the tracts or just tired of getting them, but the results were in my favor.

Tracts are messages of God's Word in a condensed form. They are mini-sermons on salvation. Carry them with you, give them out, place them in public places. We have the promise that they will not return void.

chapter six

WHEN SHALL
WE WITNESS?

I maintain that any conversation can be turned into a discussion about God. More and more people are interested in talking about what's going on in the world. They know that something is happening but they don't understand it all. They have bits and pieces of information about prophecy and the end times.

I have seen the world's attitude change drastically in the past few years with the airline industry. Several years back the airline industry as a whole was a big party group. Nowadays more and more the employees with whom I am working are concerned about their salvation. They want to know more about God and the Bible.

The same is true in other industries. Therefore we must develop the habit of daily capitalizing on any opportunity that comes our way to be an effective soulwinner.

ALTAR CALL

At the close of a service, when the invitation is given, is a very good time to open your spiritual eyes and ears to see with whom God is dealing. These people are easy to identify. They may not know our procedures—that we expect them to go down to the altar to pray. Many times I have seen sinners under conviction left standing alone while everyone else is down front. This is a very good time to whisper a prayer and ask God to give you the courage to go over and talk with this one. I have done this many times with very positive results. After a friendly greeting ask them if they understood what's going on; if not, show them in your Bible. Ask them if they would like for you to go with them down to the altar and pray. If not, would they like to pray right there?

God has already done the hard part of softening up their hearts before you got there. All you have to do is be obedient to the Spirit. I have seen many people receive the Holy Ghost right in the pews when someone prayed with them. Getting outsiders to church is the hardest part. God has already done that for you. Therefore catching these people in the pews that are already in the church and have already heard the preached Word is easy compared to catching them on the street. They will thank you for your efforts many times. I know, because this is the way that I was first led to pray in church. Thank God someone was sensitive enough to see my spiritual condition and come and pray with me.

WORKING AROUND THE ALTAR

For too long the devil has defeated us laymen with fear. I have felt this and I know that you have also. For a long time I was afraid to lay hands on someone seeking the Holy Ghost. "What if they don't receive the Holy Ghost? The pastor should be the one to pray for them," I decided. But the Bible does not require this. The busy pastor may be praying for others on the other side of the church. So we all must help him in this important task.

We must get rid of this fear. We must not be afraid to pray with and instruct people how to receive the Holy Ghost. There is only one being that does not want the candidate to receive the Holy Ghost and that is the devil. The only thing you have to do is rebuke the devil in Jesus' name and that gets rid of him very quickly. Then ask God to give you wisdom and knowledge on how to help in this important matter.

God will give you the right words to say at the right time. It's so beautiful to hear someone speaking in tongues that you have prayed for. You can experience that if you overcome the fear of failure. Let's face it; you are not going to keep him from getting the Holy Ghost if he has done God's will. You can help him receive it if you ask for God's guidance.

LETTER WRITING

Letter writing is a very effective way to witness. Look at all the letters that Paul wrote. People are thrilled to get mail. I can remember "mail call" in the Navy was an exciting time. You can be a very effective witness in your letters. It's hard to argue with the written word. The words you write are not going to change. Therefore put some truth and strength in your letters. I used this method once to explain baptism to a friend of mine. He kept changing the conversation when we talked about it; but it is impossible to change the subject of the written word. He finally read through and saw the importance of Jesus' name baptism.

TELEPHONE

The telephone is a very good tool in witnessing. "Let your fingers do the walking" to reach out to your friends and loved ones. It was by telephone that a man explained the plan of salvation to me. I did not know the full truth until this brother called me and asked me among other things, "How were you baptized?"

I said, "Just like Jesus said in Matthew 28:19."

He then explained that beautiful Scripture to me more fully. Then I saw that I needed to be baptized again. The beautiful truth of Jesus' name baptism came to me by telephone. Don't you have some important names in your address book?

BACKSLIDERS

Backsliders need a confident witness. Most backsliders that I have come in contact with know that they *should* go back to church but they feel unworthy. They feel as if God will never forgive them or they fear they cannot get back to where they once were with Him. That's a lie of the devil. Some of the finest preachers I know were backsliders at one time or another. They came back to God and He called them to preach; they now have a wonderful ministry.

A good biblical reference to bring to the backslider's attention is the story about the lost son in Luke 15. This son came back and the Father accepted him with open arms. He said, "I have sinned against heaven and in thy sight." The Father said, "He was lost and is found." This was said not to the prodigal but to the elder brother. How beautiful these words can be to a backslider.

I had the opportunity to talk with the daughter of one of our well-known and respected ministers several months ago. This beautiful girl had been away from the church for several years. The devil had dealt her many losing hands in the game of life, yet she would not come back to church. She wanted to live for God but was afraid that she would fail again. She was afraid that she would not be accepted back into the family of God.

We all know that these are lies of the devil. I talked with this girl about coming back to God, how easy it was, and how eager God was to take her back. "He's just waiting for you to say the word," I reassured her.

She really began to smile and get excited. Then the tears of repentance flowed down her cheeks as God reached down and brought her back home for good.

A year has passed now and she tells me that this has been the happiest year of her life. She is now leading others to the truth. Do you know any backsliders?

THE FIVE MOST WANTED SOULS

My pastor asked that we make a list of our five most wanted souls. He said to put this list where we could see it every day and pray for these souls to be filled with the Holy Ghost. I made my list like everyone else and put it in my billfold. My dad, my brother, my children, and a fellow employee were on the list. Within two years, four out of the five had been saved. That's not bad!

Now I have another list. I must admit I didn't have much faith in the ones on my first list being saved but somehow they were. God wanted them saved and He worked out all the impossible situations to get them in a position to call on Him. See what a small token of faith like that little list can accomplish with God's help?

Do you know five souls that you would like to see saved? Then make your list and pray for them every time you see the list. You'll be surprised at the results.

chapter seven

PERSONAL WITNESSING

Please allow me to give you some personal examples of my witnessing to others. I do not tell these different accounts to pin a crown of accomplishments on myself, nor do I relate these situations so that you might think that I am some kind of expert on the subject of soulwinning. I only give these examples because they happen to be people I was witnessing to. I am very thankful to God for allowing me to be a partner with Him on these few occasions. There have been many times that I have failed to win a soul as there have been many times that I failed to catch fish while fishing. But one thing I have found out is, if you fish long enough and look for that soul long enough you will come up with a trophy catch.

The great accomplishment of man is not the discovery of electricity, or the discovery of a vaccine for some dreaded disease, or landing a spaceship on the moon. No, greater than any other accomplishment man has achieved is that of winning a soul. It's so important that the angels in the presence of God rejoice over one soul that cometh to repentance.

Other achievements by men are usually enjoyed only by a select few scientists, doctors, or engineers. They are the only ones who have the capability and education to achieve these great tasks. However, we who have the Holy Ghost can achieve man's greatest accomplishment by just telling our friends and neighbors what God has done for us, and what great things He *can* and *wants* to do for them. We can lead them to a plan of eternal life. Doctors cannot do this, nor lawyers, nor any other group that does not have the Spirit of truth.

Not only can you lead persons to eternal life but you can also lead them to a life of peace while on this earth. You can show them how God has healed friends of cancer, heart disease, and other diseases which man cannot heal. You can show them how God has put marriages back together; broken marriages that marriage counselors could not put back together. You can show them how drug addicts have been cured, which no drying out clinic could do. You can tell them how to burst forth out of the grave on that great day, which no other power on this earth can perform. The greatest accomplishment of man is winning a soul. This is a time that man and God are teamed up together for the same goals. I have felt more anointed, felt more of the Spirit of God, more of the words of wisdom when talking with a person about Jesus than at any other time.

One prayer that God is always willing and eager to answer is the prayer of "Lord, let me witness to someone today." Before that day is out you will get your chance.

As an airline pilot, I travel to many different cities. After several hours of flying we will layover or stop for the night in a predetermined city. I was on such a trip a couple of years ago and we stopped in the city of New Orleans. We were to leave New Orleans late the next afternoon so I had some free time. I well remember sitting in my hotel room and asking the Lord to let me witness to someone that day. I thought I was safe in the request because I did not know anyone in New Orleans that I could witness to and I really had not planned to leave the room.

Later that afternoon I decided to go down to the corner drugstore for a cup of coffee. As I was walking down the street I saw a drunkard lying in the ditch alongside the road. "What a waste of a human life," I thought.

After I was in the coffee shop for about three minutes, this old drunk came in and sat down on the stool next to me. He smelled so bad that I could hardly sit there. Then he tapped me on the arm and asked if I would give him some money to buy food. "No, but I will buy you some food," I answered. I knew if I gave him money that he would probably buy more liquor. I called the waitress over and ordered this old wino something to eat.

While the food was being prepared, I felt the urge to witness to him. "This is one time I have really missed God because this old man doesn't even know that he is in the world," I thought as I glanced at the face lying on the counter. He was in a semi-passed-out condition. Yet I felt a very strong urge to talk to him about the Lord.

I began by saying, "Mister, you must have a praying mother because I feel God wants me to talk to you about Him." By this time the old man didn't even know what I was saying. I talked to him about three minutes then paid for his lunch and left. "Boy, you have really missed God this time," I thought.

63

Then I walked out on Canal Street to do some window shopping. It was just before the Christmas holidays. As I stopped in front of the first store a man approached me and asked, "What gospel do you preach?" I turned and saw a young man standing beside me. He had been in the coffee shop sitting about four stools further down the counter from me and the old drunk.

"I am not a preacher," I replied. "I am just a witness for Jesus Christ."

"I heard every word you told the old drunk fellow and I feel that the message was for me," he insisted. As yet he didn't know me from Adam and I surely didn't know him. Then the man began to empty his heart out to me about the way God had been dealing with him.

He told me that he had been raised in a United Pentecostal Church up north and had turned his back on God. Recently God had given him a vision that if he didn't get back in church he would be lost.

How shocked I was when he told me that he had been raised in a United Pentecostal Church. He also told me he had a good job with the same airline that I was working for and had gotten fired because of drinking on the job. That too got my attention.

Then I began to see how God had worked the whole thing out. The witnessing was not for the old drunk but for this young man. I am so thankful that I was obedient to the Spirit and witnessed even though I didn't feel that I was accomplishing anything. "It [my word] shall not return unto me void" (Isaiah 55:11).

I took this man up to my hotel room and prayed with him. I know the pastor in New Orleans very well so I called him and told him the story. Brother John Cupit prayed with the man on the phone and invited him to church. It was now time for me to leave New Orleans and my new-found brother.

About one year later I received a phone call from a man in Florida. I did not remember his name until he recounted the story of our meeting in New Orleans. He said the reason he was calling was again to thank me for being obedient to the Spirit and leading him back to Jesus. He said that he and his wife were back together and he had his job back and that he was in a very good United Pentecostal Church in Florida.

I prayed a simple prayer that day in New Orleans asking God to lead me to a soul. That soul was very near and God arranged all the impossible situations to get me to the backslider. There are a lot more needy souls out there that God wants us to talk with. He will arrange the situations if we are willing to witness.

That man was not the only one who prospered out of that deal. My faith increased about 1000%. This incident let me know that God *does* care for the sinner as well as the saint.

A few years ago one Thursday night the Lord impressed me to go visit my parents. I had talked with them a few days before and everything seemed to be going fine so I had not planned to visit them this particular weekend.

When my wife and I arrived at my parents' home, we discovered that my dad was very sick. He didn't know what was wrong. Neither did the doctor. All we knew was that my father was a very sick man.

My dad hardly ever went to church, but my mother always lived close to the Lord. After I received the Holy Ghost, my dad started going to Sunday school with me when I was visiting with him. I tried every way I could to get him to go to the altar and pray or make some type of move toward God. But it seemed that the more I said about it the less he was interested in the whole program. My faith for my dad to come into the church was severely tested. When I saw how sick Dad was, I made a final plea for him to make a move toward God. "Dad, God has got you in this situation for a purpose and I want to pray for you," I said. My mother and I laid hands on him and started to pray for him. Then he began to pray. In just a few moments he was speaking in tongues. A beautiful shine came upon his face and he said, "I have never felt better in my whole life, praise the Lord." How happy we were to see my dad filled with the Holy Spirit.

Three days later we had his funeral. Before my dad died he said, "Son, the reason I made the move to God was because of the change I saw in your life." Up until that point I had thought all my witnessing had been in vain, but my dad had taken in my every word and action and carefully considered the whole situation. Finally he was convinced there was something to this Holy Ghost movement. Then he asked God to forgive him and fill him with His Spirit.

That funeral was like a revival. Yes, we were heartbroken and missed him very much. Yet we were happy that God had saved him at the last hour. The ending was so beautiful. Later we learned that he had cancer. The Lord was merciful to him by saving his soul; what else could we ask for?

I must say the old enemy started to work on me soon after the funeral. He kept putting thoughts in my mind like he really didn't speak in tongues, or he really didn't do anything for God so how could you expect him to be saved? Soon I got enough of that kind of foolishness and asked God to show me some way if my dad was really saved.

In a very short period I had three dreams about my dad. In the first two dreams I saw him standing up singing and worshiping the Lord in the church. He looked great with a big smile on his face. The third dream was one that really got my attention. I dreamed that he was in a morgue and about to be embalmed. Somehow I knew that he was not dead but the undertakers didn't know that. They thought he was dead and were about to drain the blood from his body. I was struggling, like you do sometimes in a dream, trying to get to him before it was too late. Finally I reached him just seconds before they placed him in the coffin. I screamed, "He's not dead yet." I took him by the hand and he got up. The next thing I remember in the dream was that he was in the church again with a big smile as beautiful as ever.

I believe the Lord let me have that dream to show me to never give up on anyone. I had just reached my dad in time. "Lord, help me to reach others just in time!" Like the old preacher said, "Lord, put me on the one yard line of hell so that I might stop them at the last minute from entering into that terrible place."

Never give up on your dad, mother, sister, brother, son, daughter, relative, neighbor, friend, foe, or anyone within your reach. They may be watching you. That could be your best testimony, or your worst!

I owe God so much that I have to tell others. He saved my dad, mother, children, wife, friends, and me. Do you owe him anything?

67

My twin brother was really glad to hear about my conversion. He had "accepted Jesus Christ as his personal Savior" and didn't really need the Holy Ghost. When he said that, I handed him my Bible and asked him to show me where in the Bible it says to accept Jesus Christ as your personal Savior.

Well, you and I both know he couldn't find those words in the Bible because they are not in there. He said, "Well, my pastor said that's all you have to do, and besides that I have had a personal experience with God."

He was just like I was and most other people who don't read the Bible. This type of person can be led to false doctrine very easily. He began to search the Scriptures and ask God to reveal the truth to him. The Lord filled him and his wife with the Holy Ghost and they both were rebaptized into Jesus' name. They now are having Home Bible Studies and are winning souls for the kingdom of God.

Normally I fly with the same crew members for one month (captain, co-pilot, and flight engineer). One month my engineer was a very nice born again believer. I tried every way I knew to get him to see the necessity of being baptized in Jesus' name. He kept saying, "It's all semantics. When I was baptized using the words, Father, Son, and Holy Ghost, I was thinking Jesus."

The month was about over and we were on our last trip. That last flight was a late night flight from San Francisco to Dallas/Ft. Worth. The flight engineer is the crew member who normally makes the announcements to the passengers informing them of our position, altitude, speed, and other information. That clear night as we were passing over Phoenix, Arizona, this flight engineer asked me, "What city are we passing over? I need to make an announcement to the passengers."

"Doug, it really doesn't matter; they are all the same. The name is not important," I answered.

He asked again.

"Just call it a city, village, town, hamlet, or community, *the name is not* important," I insisted.

Then he got the true meaning of the importance of a name. "The name really does make a difference. I see it now," he decided.

We landed at Dallas/Fort Worth Airport about midnight, and he made me wake up my pastor to baptize him that very night. I knew my pastor wouldn't mind at all.

I am thankful that God loved that boy enough to give me the words to say which would open his heart to understand the Scriptures.

A very nice young man came to my home to test drive a car I had advertised for sale. While sitting in his car I saw that he had a crucifix on the dashboard. It was of an old man and a dog. I asked him, "Sir, what is the purpose of the old man and the dog?"

"Oh, that is St. Lazarus. You know the poor man in the Bible that had to eat crumbs from the rich man's table, and the dog licked his sores," he replied.

I had heard the story but said, "Why do you have this in your car?"

"I pray to St. Lazarus every day because he did a great favor for my family a few years ago." That opened the door for me to start telling him about the only Savior by which we can be saved.

"Sir, when you talk to me about Jesus and receiving the Holy Ghost, it makes cold chills go all over me." Since

I could tell the man was very sincere, I explained the full plan of salvation. That very day he was baptized in Jesus' name. Since that day, his wife, his daughter, his two brothers, his mother, one sister-in-law, and one of his employees are now in the church and are leading others to the truth.

See what one small witness can do?

Here is another example of personal witnessing. One Wednesday night at the close of a church service, the pastor called everyone up front and asked us to personally challenge God about soulwinning. I went up like everyone else and said my little prayer hurriedly so I could leave and get something to eat. Well, while I was down at that altar, God really impressed me to drive to my hometown in Louisiana (about 250 miles away). I didn't want to go there at that time because my wife and I had planned a trip to Mexico the next day. But the conviction was so strong to go to my home in Louisiana that I told my wife we would have to cancel the Mexico trip and go to Louisiana the next day. I really didn't know why or for whom, but I knew the Lord wanted me to go to Louisiana.

The next day I waited around until very late before starting the trip because I really didn't want to go. Finally we left Texas and arrived in Louisiana about 11 P.M. When we arrived at my mother's home, my cousin from California was there.

I had not seen her in years and hardly knew who she was. We began talking at the dinner table and she began to explain how great a life she was leading in California. She was there smoking a cigarette, with a face full of makeup, and pants so tight she could hardly breathe telling me how great the party life was in California.

Well, I heard all I wanted to hear about her party life so I began to witness to her about Jesus Christ. I told her how great a life I was having since turning my life over to Jesus. It was just plain simple talk knowing that "If I [Jesus] be lifted up . . . will draw all men unto me" (John 12:32).

Big tears began to flow and make large tracks down each side of her face through the makeup. Then she really began to pour her heart out to me and said that she was living a miserable life and needed something. She was addicted to several kinds of medicine, couldn't sleep, and was a nervous wreck. "I need God," she cried. So I began to explain the plan of salvation to her. She was a member of a charismatic church that had very few standards. In fact, her husband wouldn't go to church with her because he said that it was no more than a fashion show.

When my cousin heard my testimony and saw the truth in the Bible, she said that she must be baptized in Jesus' name. It was now about 12:30 A.M. I tried to get her to wait until morning but she said to call the preacher now and see if he would baptize her. I called the local minister and, of course, he and his wife were eager to get up and meet us at the church.

As we walked into the church at 1:00 A.M. that morning, this girl received the Holy Ghost while walking down the aisle.

Then we started running water in the baptistry in order to baptize her. After about an hour we noticed that the water was only two inches deep. Then we discovered that someone had left the stopper out of the baptistry so we had to sit there another hour to get enough water to do the job. We were all tired by this time, but we had added another soul to the Kingdom of God by sunrise.

This girl went back to California and we soon received reports that her husband and three daughters had received the Holy Ghost and had been baptized. They were Catholic. Now they are all in a good church and are doing the work of the Lord. You see how God works! He was so interested in this girl and her family that he impressed me to go, to a place I didn't want to go to, to do a job that I was not aware of. I was only obedient about going. He had already set the stage for me to act whenever I arrived there. I am just thankful that he used me. That surely was more rewarding than going to Mexico.

A couple of years back, while flying up the east coast of the United States, a flight attendant came into the cockpit to bring us something to drink. I noticed she had a dove on her uniform. I knew what the dove represented but I wanted to find out how much she knew. So I asked her, "What is the purpose of the dove?"

"Oh, that's the Holy Spirit, the third person in the Holy Trinity," she said. "I've recently been born again and I have seen the Holy Spirit do many great works," she added.

I could have said "Praise the Lord! Glad to hear the good news," but I didn't want this lady to know only half the truth. We soon landed and I had a chance to talk with her about the full plan of salvation. She had never heard of the Scriptures that I showed her concerning salvation. She called up another flight attendant that had also recently been "born again" and asked me to repeat the plan of salvation to her. I saw that these girls were very hungry for more truth.

My wife and I talked the situation over and decided to go to their city on our vacation to tell the girls more about Jesus. We called the local pastor of a United Pentecostal

Church and told him the story. He planned special services while we were in town. The girls and their families came to these services at our invitation. At last count eleven of that group were baptized in Jesus' name.

See what one small witness can do!

I have given you these personal experiences to show you that God is interested in the lost, and if we are willing and obedient, He will use us in presenting the truth to hungry souls.

The following story was told to me by a preacher friend. He said that in his early ministry he had to work in order to support his family. His church was very small and so was the income, so he got a job in a local department store to supplement his income. "Early one morning an old gentleman came into the department store and just kinda followed me around all day long," he began to relate. "Every step I took he would be there, every time I turned around he would be there. I asked him many times if I could help him find anything but he said no. The old man really got on my nerves. I got tired of seeing him and he was really in my way. I was even rude to him, hoping this would make him move on, but it didn't. Just before closing time the old man walked out of the department store. The old man only got about ten feet outside the door and fell dead of a heart attack. Then I realized that God had placed this old gentleman there for me to witness to. Yet I never said one word to him all day long about God."

This minister told me that he went to that funeral and wept more than any of the family because he didn't tell the old man about Jesus.

"I had all day to tell him about God," he said, "but I

was too busy trying to make a little money." That was many years ago but it's still fresh on this minister's heart. He told me, "Ron, don't ever pass up the opportunity to witness. You may never get the chance again."

You grow in ability every time you witness. The more you witness the more you enjoy witnessing and the more you want to witness. It becomes like a game of chess after a while. Every move the opposition makes, you contest him with more truth. You don't have to back down from anyone because truth is on your side. You just need to know the moves to make to convey that powerful truth. An example of this very important game for eternal life is in the next chapter on examples of witnessing.

chapter eight

EXAMPLE OF WITNESSING

The following is a typical example of the questions and preconceived ideas that you will encounter when witnessing to people today. I would like to share one such case with you.

Ron: *Hello, Bob, my name is Ron. It's my privilege to discuss the Bible with you today. Before we get started I want to challenge you not to take my word for anything I say. Don't take my pastor's word or anyone else's word about this important matter. Take the Word of God. If I cannot back up what I say with the Bible, then disregard what I am telling you. Therefore let the Bible be the judge.*
    Bob, do you believe in the Bible?
Bob: *Yes, sir, I do, Ron.*
Ron: *Do you believe it's the Word of God?*
Bob: *Yes. I certainly do!*
Ron: *Do you believe in God?*

Bob: *Yes, sir.*

Ron: *Do you believe that God has made provisions for man to be saved?*

Bob: *I do.*

Ron: *Bob, please tell me what you believe as far as the plan of salvation is concerned.*

Bob: *Well, Ron, it's like this. I accepted Jesus Christ as my personal Savior many years ago. You know the Bible says that we only have to confess Christ before men and we are forever saved. The Bible also says that we can't get good enough to be saved. All we need is Jesus Christ plus nothing, minus nothing. In other words we do not have to work to be saved. Jesus did all the work when He died. Some religious groups are teaching that you have to be baptized, that you have to commit time and money and a lot of other effort in order to be saved. Jesus did all the work when He died.*

Some groups even teach that you can backslide or be lost once you are saved. I wouldn't serve a God that couldn't keep me from being lost again. How can you become unborn once you have been born again?

Another thing that some churches teach is that we are still under the Law—that you must obey many different rules and regulations in order to be saved. They say you must be holy to be saved. My pastor says that no one is holy. Our sins cannot be counted against us because we have accepted Christ. He says our flesh can sin but our spirit cannot sin because we have invited Christ into our spirit. Therefore no fleshly sin will be charged against us.

There's a lot I don't know about the Bible. I do want to know more. There seems to be something missing in my relationship with God. I pray, I go to church, I have done all my pastor asks me to do. I can't really put my finger on the problem. I am sure it's just my lack of faith in certain areas.

I hear of all the healings and exciting things God is doing in other churches. Why don't we have those miracles in my church?

Ron: Bob, it's apparent that you are a sincere man wanting to do what is right in the sight of God. It is so very important to do the will of God and not the will of man or an organization.

There is a verse in Luke that shows where Jesus opened the understanding of His disciples that they might understand the Scriptures. The Bible also challenges us as Christians to "search the scriptures; for in them ye think ye have eternal life" (John 5:39).

Bob, this is such an important meeting here today so let's ask God to open our hearts to understand the Scriptures and if we lack anything according to His will and Word, please have Him reveal it to us.

"Jesus, I come to You today asking You once again to reveal the truth to us concerning our salvation. Don't let us be deceived, Lord. Don't let us be like that group in Matthew that You will tell to depart from You for You never knew them. Yet they thought they were doing Your will. Please don't *allow us to believe a lie and be damned, but open our hearts to understand the Scriptures so that 10,000 years from now we will be in your glorious presence. I ask it all in Jesus' name. Amen."*

Bob, the Lord is in this conversation today. The Bible says where two or three are gathered together in His name, there will He be in the midst of them.

First of all, you told me that you had accepted Jesus Christ as your personal Savior. Would you please show me in the Bible the verse of Scripture that commands us to accept Jesus Christ as our personal Savior and by doing so we are saved?

Bob: *Well, I really don't know where it is in the Bible, but I know it's in there because my pastor said it was.*

Ron: *Bob, let's see what the Bible really says. I hung my salvation on what other people said until I found out they were not telling me the full truth.*

Let's turn in our Bibles to Romans 10:9. This verse says, "That if thou shalt confess with thy mouth the Lord Jesus, and shalt believe in thine heart that God hath raised him from the dead, thou shalt be saved."

The first time that I ever made any sort of move toward God a minister read me that verse. He then asked me if I believed the Bible. I said yes. Then he pronounced me saved. I said, "Sir, I don't feel any different." He said, "Salvation doesn't come by feelings but by faith." He again assured me that I couldn't ever be anymore saved than I was at the moment. Bob, my problem was I didn't know anything about the Bible

That preacher pulled that verse out of context and built a church on it. That's like quoting the Scripture, "Jesus wept," and believe that all He did for 33 years was bawl and squall, or that He was a big cry baby. If I had only known enough to read the rest of that chapter it would have told me what to do.

Look at Romans 10:13: "For whosoever shall call upon the name of the Lord shall be saved." Many churches have stopped there and built a doctrine that all you have to do is quote that verse to be saved. Let's keep reading. Look at the warnings to come in the next few verses. "How then shall they call on him in whom they have not believed? and how shall they believe in him of whom they have not heard? and how shall they hear without a preacher? And how shall they preach, except they be sent? as it is written, How beautiful are the feet of them that preach the gospel of peace, and bring glad tidings of good things! But they have not all obeyed the gospel. For Esaias saith, Lord, who hath believed our report? So then faith cometh by hearing, and hearing by the word of God" (Romans 10:13-17).

Now let's go back and look at those verses of Scripture again real close. Notice that the Lord gives us a warning that all have not obeyed the gospel; also, notice that faith cometh by hearing and hearing by the Word of God. In other words, for me to have faith in the Bible I have to know what it says; not what some man says it says. I

79

have faith that the cover of this Bible I hold in my hand is black because I have been taught all the colors since childhood and this one has all the characteristics of being black. Do you understand that, Bob?

Bob: Well, I guess so. I know one thing for sure. I believe in God.

Ron: I don't doubt that in the least. But again let's go to the Bible and see what it says about a believer. James 2:19 says that the devils believe in one God, they believe it so strong that they tremble. Do you think the devils are saved?

Bob: No.

Ron: Let's see what Jesus said would be the signs of the believer. Flip over to John 7:38-39.

Bob: Where?

Ron: John 7:38-39. Yeah, right there. The red letter part. Read that for me please.

Bob: "He that believeth on me, as the scripture hath said, out of his belly shall flow rivers of living water. (But this spake he of the Spirit, which they that believe on him should receive: for the Holy Ghost was not yet given; because that Jesus was not yet glorified)."

Ron: Jesus clearly says in that passage that the believer would receive the Holy Ghost if he believed as the Scripture says. I didn't receive the Holy Ghost when my pastor read Romans 10:9 to me. Something was not complete. Let's look at another verse concerning what believers do. Please read Mark 16:16-17.

Bob: "He that believeth and is baptized shall be

saved; but he that believeth not shall be damned. And these signs shall follow them that believe; In my name shall they cast out devils; they shall speak with new tongues."

Ron: *Bob, there is even more evidence of what a believer must do according to Jesus. They must be baptized and speak with new tongues. My pastor didn't tell me this when he read Romans 10:9 to me.*

Bob: *Ron, are you trying to tell me that I am not saved?*

Ron: *Bob, it's not my place to judge anyone. In fact, the Bible says, "Judge not lest ye be judged." You are the one reading the Scriptures. I just wanted to show you what Jesus had to say about your salvation. It's up to you to obey the Scriptures. Please don't take my word for anything that I can not back up in the Bible.*

Bob: *Will you tell me of your plan of salvation?*

Ron: *Bob, I don't have a plan of salvation. I just try to obey the one that God laid down for mankind. Ephesians 4:5 says there is "one Lord, one faith, one baptism." Paul said in Galatians 1:8, "But though we, or an angel from heaven, preach any other gospel unto you than that which we have preached unto you, let him be accursed." Paul felt so strongly about this that he repeated himself in the next verse.*

Bob: *What did they preach?*

Ron: *The same message that the Lord sent on the Day of Pentecost. That is, to repent, be baptized in Jesus' name and receive the Holy Ghost.*

81

Bob: The thief on the cross didn't do all of that and he was saved.

Ron: That's a very good point. Let's look at the Bible again for the answer.

First of all, we need to divide the Bible into proper order. Note the four Gospels: Matthew, Mark, Luke, and John. These are the books of history. They tell about His birth, ministry, death, and resurrection. Then we have the Book of Acts. This is where the church was born and the church age started. Most denominations will agree about this point. Then we have the epistles or letters written to the established church on how to conduct their services, how to live as Christians, family life, and other Christian principles. These books are Romans through Jude. Then, of course, there is Revelation. That is prophecy.

Our plan of salvation is not found in Matthew, Mark, Luke, or John because Jesus had not died yet for our sins. Remember in John 7:39 Jesus said the Holy Ghost would not come until He died?

Therefore this thief on the cross died prior to the establishment of the New Testament church, or under a different dispensation. I believe that he is saved. But what did Jesus tell us to do?

Bob: Well, it says in John 3:16, "For God so loved the world, that he gave his only begotten Son, that whosoever believeth in him should not perish, but have everlasting life."

Ron: Bob, I think we covered the signs of a true believer earlier in this discussion.

82

Do you still maintain all you have to do is say I believe?

Bob: No, I don't guess; but, boy, I am getting confused.

Ron: *I know exactly how you feel. One day I was sitting on your side of the table wanting to know more truth, but it was very hard to erase all the things I had been taught in my church.*

Let's get right to the point and see what Jesus told His disciples to do just prior to His ascension into heaven. Don't you think His last instructions to His people would be very important?

Bob: *Yes.*

Ron: *Flip over to Luke 24 and read verses 45, 47, and 49.*

Bob: *"Then opened he their understanding, that they might understand the scriptures . . . And that repentance and remission of sins should be preached in his name among all nations, beginning at Jerusalem . . . And, behold, I send the promise of my Father upon you: but tarry ye in the city of Jerusalem, until ye be endued with power from on high."*

Ron: Okay, hold your fingers on the page and let's turn over to Acts 1:4 and see if these disciples obeyed Jesus. See there in the fourth verse they are retelling what Jesus told them. He commanded them not to depart from Jerusalem but wait for the promise of the Father. Verse five tells us that this promise was the Holy Ghost. This was not available to the thief on the cross or to anyone else until the Father sent the Holy Ghost.

This little book I hold in my hand is a legal instrument, it is a testament. What must happen before a testament becomes effective? Of course, the testator must die. Read Hebrews 9:16-17, please.

Bob: *"For where a testament is, there must also of necessity be the death of the testator. For a testament is of force after men are dead: otherwise it is of no strength at all while the testator liveth."*

Ron: *Bob, do you see now why Jesus had to die in order for us to have the Holy Ghost? He said back in John 14:18, "I will not leave you comfortless: I will come to you." John 14:26 says, "But the Comforter, which is the Holy Ghost, whom the Father will send in my name, he shall teach you all things. . . ." The Holy Ghost is Jesus' Spirit; it can be with everyone all over the world at the same time. Acts 5:32 says that God will give the Holy Ghost to those who obey him.*

Now I want you to read Acts 2:1-4. But first let me tell you or show you in the Bible what was taking place.

First we see that the disciples obeyed Jesus. They went to Jerusalem and up into the upper room and continued in prayer and supplication. There were about 120 disciples in this group. This was on a Jewish holiday called Pentecost. Pentecost means fifty in Greek and this was fifty days after the Passover holiday. Please read Acts 2:1-4.

Bob: *"And when the day of Pentecost was fully come, they were all with one accord in one place. And suddenly there came a sound from heaven as of a rushing mighty wind, and it filled all the house where they were sitting. And there appeared unto them cloven tongues like as of fire, and it sat upon each of them. And they were all filled with the Holy Ghost, and began to speak with other tongues, as the Spirit gave them utterance."*

Ron: *You can read the rest of that chapter and see that some people thought these men and women were drunk or crazy. But Peter told them this was not the case. He quoted an Old Testament prophet, Joel, who said this would happen.*

Then they asked Peter, "What shall we do?" Bob, read Acts 2:38.

Bob: *"Then Peter said unto them, Repent, and be baptized every one of you in the name of Jesus Christ for the remission of sins, and ye shall receive the gift of the Holy Ghost."*

Ron: *Bob, you asked earlier what was my plan of salvation. What you just read is God's plan of salvation for the whole world. I would now like to take the Bible and prove to you without any doubt that this is God's plan to redeem mankind. First of all let's stop and get a fresh cup of coffee. How do you like yours?*

Bob: *Cream and sugar please.*

Ron: *Remember earlier I told you to hold your finger at Luke 24:47-49. Let's go back there now and see if Peter obeyed Jesus' command in Acts 2:38. But first let's look at Peter's authority, and why the others asked him, "What must we do?" Please read Matthew 16:19.*

Bob: "And I will give unto thee the keys of the kingdom of heaven: and whatsoever thou shalt bind
on earth shall be bound in heaven: and whatsoever thou shalt loose on earth shall be loosed in
heaven."

Ron: So we can see in that Scripture and the one
above it, that Peter would be given the keys to the
kingdom of heaven.

Again let's look at Luke 24:47. Jesus said that,
"Repentance and remission of sins should be
preached in his name . . . beginning at Jerusalem."

Peter said in Acts 2:38 to repent; that is step
number one. He said to be baptized in Jesus'
name for the remission of sins, and ye shall
receive the gift of the Holy Ghost. Bob, do you
know the difference between repentance of sins
and remission of sin?

Bob: Well, Ron, I kind of thought they were the same
thing.

Ron: Let me give you an example. Suppose you
spilled that cup of coffee on my new carpet. I am
sure you would say, "Oh, I am very sorry, Ron,
please forgive me." I would forgive you, but the
coffee would still be in the carpet. It must be
washed away somehow or remitted, or else it
will leave a bad stain on the carpet.

Now I think you can see why we must be baptized in Jesus' name for the remission of sins. This
is applying His precious blood to our tarnished
life and removing our sin forever. The Bible says
we must be without spot or wrinkle to enter in.
Only the blood of Jesus Christ can remit sin. Not

86

the blood of bulls or goats, but the blood of God. That's the reason Jesus had to die, to shed His blood, and by being baptized in His name we are applying that blood to our lives. Read Acts 20:28 please.

Bob: *"Take heed therefore unto yourselves, and to all the flock, over the which the Holy Ghost hath made you overseers, to feed the church of God, which he hath purchased with his own blood."*

Ron: *God purchased the church with his own blood. Now read Romans 3:25.*

Bob: *"Whom God hath set forth to be a propitiation through faith in his blood, to declare his right-eousness for the remission of sins that are past, through the forbearance of God."*

Ron: *We must have faith in the shedding of Jesus' blood, which is the same as God's blood. Now read Hebrews 9:22.*

Bob: *"And almost all things are by the law purged with blood; and without shedding of blood is no remission."*

Ron: *Bob, I hope you can see how important this remission and shedding of blood is. This is the only legal way that God could redeem or buy back man after the fall in the Garden. The blood of God will remit sins forever. Like the Bible says in I Corinthians 6:20, "For ye are bought with a price." Therefore we apply His blood in baptism in His name, that is Jesus' name. Colossians 2:12 says we are buried with Him in baptism and we rise to a new life. That's what is meant by being "born again," not shaking some preacher's hand.*

Jesus said in John 3:5, "Except a man be born of water and of the Spirit, he cannot enter into the kingdom of God."

Bob: *Ron, let me tell you what I have been taught about baptism. First of all my pastor says it's only an outward profession for an inward possession. It's good to follow Christ in baptism but it's not necessary for salvation. He also says he had rather follow the words of Jesus in Matthew 28:19 and baptize in the name of the Father, Son and Holy Ghost than the words of Peter. He says that baptism was important in those days as a public example that the Jews had accepted Jesus as their personal Savior, but it's not that important today.*

Ron: *Bob, my ex-pastor told me that exact same thing, but again let's read God's Word on this subject. Please read I Peter 3:21.*

Bob: *"The like figure whereunto even baptism doth also now save us (not the putting away of the filth of the flesh, but the answer of a good conscience toward God,) by the resurrection of Jesus Christ."*

Ron: *Do you see in that where it says water baptism saves us?*

Bob: *Yes, that's sure what it says.*

Ron: *We can see in Acts 22:16 where baptism washed away the sins of the apostle Paul. Please read that.*

Bob: *"And now why tarriest thou? arise, and be baptized, and wash away thy sins, calling on the name of the Lord.*

Ron: *There are many other verses of Scripture that*

we could use to prove the importance of baptism. Do you understand now that the Bible says we must be baptized?

Bob: *Yes, I do, Ron. I forgot to tell you in the beginning of this discussion that I have already been baptized.*

Ron: *Bob, if you were baptized like you said your pastor believed, then you were not baptized like the Bible says. Please give me a little time to explain this very important procedure. I too was once baptized in the titles of the Father, Son and Holy Ghost. Yet when I asked God for more truth, He showed me that I must be baptized in Jesus' name. The only example ever used in the Bible is baptism in Jesus' name.*

Bob: *What about Matthew 28:19?*

Ron: *Good point, Bob. Let's look at that beautiful commission from Jesus. Please read it.*

Bob: *"Go ye therefore, and teach all nations, baptizing them in the name of the Father, and of the Son, and of the Holy Ghost." See it says it right there. My pastor was right!*

Ron: *Bob, I know that you were in the Marines and I know that they taught you commands. A good example is the command "Forward, march." Remember how the drill instructor used to tell us that the command "Forward" was a preparatory command and the word "March" was the execution command? Remember how they used to try to get us to err by saying "Forward," and not saying "March"? We would lean forward or take that first step, then really get chewed out because we didn't wait for the command, "March." Or remember the command "About, face." He would sometimes say "About" and some of us would turn around before he said, "Face." Of course, this was wrong.*

Bob: *How well do I remember those days!*

Ron: *This command that Jesus gave in Matthew 28:19 was as a preparatory command. The command of execution came in Acts 2:38 when the words in the name of Jesus were given.*

In other words, your minister just repeated the words of Jesus; he really didn't complete the command.

Let me give another example. I want you to repeat the words I say. Bob, go close the door.

Bob: *Bob, go close the door.*

Ron: *You see you really have not done anything. The door is still open and you have not moved one inch. Was that obeying my command?*

Bob: *No, but how does that tie in with what Jesus said?*

Ron: *The point is this: Jesus gave the command and the disciples understood it. Remember He opened their understanding, and they obeyed His command in Acts 2:38.*

There are no contradictions in the Bible. Did Jesus and Peter say the same thing? Let's look at that point very closely. To understand this command we must find out the name of the Father, Son and Holy Ghost. Then we must apply that name to Jesus' command. You see the name is singular, so it's one name.

Please read Matthew 1:21 to find out the name of the Son.

Bob: *"And she shall bring forth a son, and thou shalt call his name JESUS."*

Ron: *The son's name is Jesus. Now let's find out the name of the Holy Ghost. Please read the words of Jesus in John 14:26.*

Bob: *"But the Comforter, which is the Holy Ghost, whom the Father will send in my name."*

Ron: *So the name of the Holy Ghost is Jesus. Now let's find out the name of the Father. Please read the words of Jesus in John 5:43.*

Bob: *"I am come in my Father's name."*

Ron: *You see, Bob, that the name of the Father, Son and Holy Ghost is Jesus. That's the reason there was no great discussion on the Day of Pentecost when Peter commanded them all to be baptized in the name of Jesus Christ. Brother Matthew was there that day; you can find him on the roster in the thirteenth verse of Acts, the first chapter. Why didn't he jump up and say, "Brother Peter, you got it all wrong. That's not the way I am going to write it in my book." The reason is they knew who Jesus was—God with us. Remember He opened their understanding.*

Bob: *Ron, why haven't I been taught that in my church? My pastor has a doctor's degree in Bible studies, a graduate of the finest seminary, yet I have never heard that before.*

Ron: *Bob, if you don't mind we'll cover that subject later. I want to tell you this, that the doctrine of the Holy Trinity is not found in the Bible, and this is where the practice of baptism using the words Father, Son and Holy Ghost got started. This was first accepted at the Council of Nicea, about 325 years after the death of Jesus Christ.*

There is only one God; not three. He has only one name and that name is Jesus. Acts 4:12 says, "Neither is there salvation in any other: for there is none other name under heaven given among men, whereby we must be saved."

Bob: *What about the Son of God? Who did Jesus pray to? Who raised Jesus from the dead? Where was God when Jesus was a baby?*

Ron: *Bob, those are very good questions and in order to give you a good answer we again must turn to the Word of God. This might take a while so we might better get another fresh cup of coffee.*

Read Deuteronomy 6:4. I like to call this the $64 question of the Bible.

Bob: *"Hear, O Israel: The LORD our God is one LORD."*

Ron: *Please read Isaiah 9:6.*

Bob: *"For unto us a child is born, unto us a son is given: and the government shall be upon his shoulder: and his name shall be called Wonderful, Counsellor, The mighty God, The everlasting Father, The Prince of Peace."*

Ron: *Do you see, Bob, that this child is the Son and the everlasting Father, the Mighty God? Wonderful is not His name. But Jesus is a wonderful name. All of these are one.*

Now turn to Isaiah 43:10-11 and let's see who God and Savior is. Also Isaiah 45:5.

Bob: *I guess you want me to read that too!*

Ron: *Yes, you are doing a super job.*

Bob: *"Ye are my witnesses, saith the LORD, and my servant whom I have chosen: that ye may know and believe me, and understand that I am he: before me there was no God formed, neither shall there be after me. I, even I, am the LORD; and beside me there is no saviour." Isaiah 45:5, "I am the LORD, and there is none else, there is no God beside me."*

Ron, that's pretty plain; there is only one God.

Ron: *There are many other verses of Scripture to show that fact. Read who Jesus said He was in Revelation 1:8.*

Bob: *"I am Alpha and Omega, the beginning and the ending, saith the Lord, which is, and which was, and which is to come, the Almighty."*

Ron: *Jesus says He is the Almighty God. He says again in Revelation 21:6 that He is the Alpha and the Omega, also in Revelation 22:13.*

Bob: *You still haven't answered my questions on who Jesus prayed to, who raised Him from the dead and where was God when Jesus was a child.*

Ron: *Well, let me answer them in another way. I believe that you see now that there is only one God.*

Bob: *Yes, I do.*

Ron: *Praise the Lord. This is a beautiful revelation. Let's took at I Timothy 3:16 and see what a beautiful mystery that God has revealed to you. Please read it.*

Bob: *"And without controversy great is the mystery*

93

of godliness: God was manifest in the flesh, justi-
fied in the Spirit, seen of angels, preached unto
the Gentiles, believed on in the world, received up
into glory."

Ron: *You see, Bob, Jesus had a dual nature when He*
was here on this earth. He was both man and
God. He was man when He fasted, when He
prayed, when He wept, when He slept, when He
ate and when He did all the other things that are
natural to the flesh. He was our example but
without sin. The flesh died on the cross.

He was God when He performed the many mir-
acles such as walking on the water, turning the
water into wine, and when He raised Himself
from the dead. He told His disciples, "Destroy this
temple and in three days I will raise it up.

You will never find eternal Sonship taught in
the Bible! That which was conceived, or begot-
ten, the flesh, had a beginning and an ending, but
the Spirit has always been.

It's unfortunate that the church world has
watered down the deity of Jesus Christ, making
Him one of three Gods. He is not one of three; He
is the only one in three manifestations.

I don't think it would take three Gods to defeat
one Satan, do you? Jesus is Almighty. He has
taken power over death, hell and the grave.

Bob: *I see your point.*

Ron: *Praise the Lord. Now, Bob, I want to show you*
how to receive His Spirit. There are many ex-
amples of this in the Bible. Let's turn back to Acts
2:4.

94

Bob: *You mean speaking in tongues? Well, my pastor covered that point very thoroughly last week. He said these Pentecostal groups were trying to cause confusion in the major denominations by this tongues doctrine.*

     He said that he believed the account in the first part of Acts that the Jews spoke in tongues, but that was a special language gift so that they could be missionaries in foreign lands. He said that this gift was only for the Jews, and it was not for Christians today.

Ron: *I sure would like to meet that pastor of yours sometime. I think we could have a great discussion on this subject.*

     Bob, again let's go to the Word of God for the answers to this very important question. I would like to say that if God used tongues in Acts the second chapter as a special missionary gift, why hasn't He used it since then for that same purpose? Our missionaries of today sure could save a lot of time and study learning the language of the people they are sent to if this were the case. God uses this great event today as He did on the Day of Pentecost to show that man has truly obeyed Him and that He, God, the Spirit, is taking residence in this man's soul. God's Spirit is speaking through this man in a language unknown to him. This is the evidence of the Holy Ghost. The Bible says in Corinthians, "Tongues are for a sign." The Bible also says in James "the tongue can no man tame," but God can when He moves into man's soul.

95

Please read Acts 2:4.

Bob: "And they were all filled with the Holy Ghost, and began to speak with other tongues, as the Spirit gave them utterance."

Ron: Here, read it in the New International Version.

Bob: "All of them were filled with the Holy Spirit and began to speak in other tongues as the Spirit enabled them."

Ron: Let's see who some of these people were. The Bible named a few of the first tongue talkers. Read the roster in Acts 1:13.

Bob: Peter, James, John, Andrew, Philip, Thomas, Bartholomew, Matthew, James, Simon, Judas, the brother of James.

Ron: Very select group, wouldn't you say? Even Mary the mother of Jesus was listed with the women in the next verse.

Bob: She sure was!

Ron: Peter told these people, "This is that which was spoken by the prophet Joel." He also said, "The promise is for you and your children and for all who are afar off—for all whom the Lord our God will call." Not just for the Jews or the missionaries.

Bob, please turn to Acts chapter 10 and read the second verse.

Bob: "A devout man, and one that feared God with all his house, which gave much alms to the people, and prayed to God alway."

Ron: This man was an Italian, a Gentile. I would think according to that second verse that he could be in the "Amen Corner" of any church. He could be a Sunday school teacher, minister, or just *about anything because of his devotion. Yet according to the Bible he was not saved.*

Bob: *Where does it say that?*

Ron: *I'll show you in a few minutes. First let's notice that this man was sincere with God. God honored his sincerity and sent a man to talk to him. Not an angel, not a loud voice from heaven but a man.*

When I was sincere with God, He sent a man to talk with me about what I must do. We see in the thirty-third verse that Cornelius sent for Peter to listen to everything the Lord had commanded him to do.

Remember the great commandment that the Lord gave to Peter which was fulfillment of the great commission?

Bob: *Yes, that was Acts 2:38.*

Ron: *Right, so read Acts 10:44-47 please.*

Bob: *"While Peter yet spake these words, the Holy Ghost fell on all them which heard the word. And they of the circumcision which believed were astonished, as many as came with Peter, because that on the Gentiles also was poured out the gift of the Holy Ghost."*

Ron: *Bob, stop right there for a minute. How did they know that Cornelius and his people received the Holy Ghost?*

Bob: *Well, it says in the next verse that they heard them speak with tongues and magnify God!*

Ron: *They heard them do what?*

Bob: *Speak in tongues!*

Ron: *You mean just like Peter and his group did on the Day of Pentecost?*

Bob: Must be the same because they said in the next verse, "Can any man forbid water, that these should not be baptized, which have received the Holy Ghost as well as we?"

Ron: How were they baptized? Was it in the name of the Father, Son and Holy Ghost?

Bob: No, the Bible says in this New International Version, verse 48, "So he ordered that they be baptized in the name of Jesus Christ."

Ron: Well, isn't that just like the Lord, to let us Gentiles have the Holy Ghost just like the Jews. I guess He gave it to the Italians next because there were no Texans around at that time. Ha!

Bob: What about me? I am from the north.

Ron: Well, it took awhile longer for you Yankees. We see an example of that in Acts the nineteenth chapter. Paul found them while passing through the upper coast. Do you suppose the upper coast was Yankee country? Read what Paul asked these souls in verse two.

Bob: "He said unto them, Have ye received the Holy Ghost since ye believed? And they said unto him, We have not so much as heard whether there be any Holy Ghost?"

Ron: Keep reading.

Bob: "And he said unto them, Unto what then were ye baptized? And they said, Unto John's baptism."

Ron: Keep reading.

Bob: "Then said Paul, John verily baptized with the baptism of repentance, saying unto the people, that they should believe on him which should come after him, that is, on Christ Jesus."

Ron: *Keep reading.*

Bob: "When they heard this, they were baptized in the name of the Lord Jesus."

Ron: *You mean to tell me that these people were rebaptized? They had already been baptized by John.*

Bob: *Don't take my word for it; that's what the Bible says.*

Ron: *Super. Well, what else happened?*

Bob: *Verse six says, "And when Paul had laid his hands upon them, the Holy Ghost came on them."*

Ron: How *did they know they received the Holy Ghost?*

Bob: *The Bible says they spoke with tongues.*

Ron: *Well, those people from the upper coast got the Holy Ghost and spoke with tongues. Brother Peter was right when he said it's for all, even to those who are afar* off.

Bob: *Sure looks that way.*

Ron: *What about you, Bob? Have you received the Holy Ghost since you believed with the evidence of speaking in tongues?*

Bob: *Ron, the Bible does not say that everyone that received the Holy Ghost spoke with tongues. In fact Paul said, "I had rather speak five words with my understanding than ten thousand words in an unknown tongue." Why would he make such a statement if tongues are that important?*

Ron: *"Jesus wept!" Remember the example I used in the beginning of this discussion about taking Scriptures out of context? The one you just quoted is a classic example of taking a verse out of context. Let's let the Bible answer that for us.*

First I want to go on record here and now and say I don't think anyone should seek to speak in tongues. Did any of the people in the examples we saw in the Bible seek tongues? No. They were seeking the Holy Ghost, the Spirit of God, and the tongues came as evidence that they had received the Spirit. When you go to buy a pair of shoes, do you ask for a pair of size ten tongues? Of course not, you ask for the shoes and the tongues come with them. You ask God for the Holy Ghost and the tongues come with the Spirit.

Bob: *Why did Paul say what he said about speaking in tongues then?*

Ron: *Remember earlier when we talked about rightly dividing the Word of God? You are jumping over I Corinthians the fourteenth chapter and are talking about an event that has nothing to do with receiving the gift of the Holy Ghost. Please let me explain.*

Bob: *Please do.*

Ron: *Look back at Acts and you will see that these people received the gift of the Holy Ghost, not the gift of tongues. When they received this precious gift they all spoke with tongues. We have already covered that point very well.*

Now let's go to I Corinthians the twelfth chapter and read about the nine spiritual gifts, one of which is the gift of many kinds of tongues.

Read I Corinthians 12:8 through 10 please.

Bob: *"For to one is given by the Spirit the word of*

100

wisdom; to another the word of knowledge by the same Spirit; to another faith by the same Spirit; to another the gifts of healing by the same Spirit; to another the working of miracles; to another prophecy; to another discerning of spirits; to another divers kinds of tongues; to another the interpretation of tongues."

Ron: *Bob, these are the nine spiritual gifts of the Bible. I do not have any of them. Yet when I received the Holy Ghost I spoke in tongues. Do you see the difference?*

Bob: *Well, I guess so.*

Ron: *Don't guess about it. Let's dig further into the Word of God. I know how you feel because I was told that tongues would cease, that Paul didn't like tongues, that prophecy was greater than tongues, that all do not speak with tongues and so on.*

  Remember we are dealing with a gift of the church. This was so important that God wrote about how to use this gift in three chapters of His precious Book.

  I had people lead me to I Corinthians 13:8-10 and quote, "Whether there be tongues, they shall cease." Read the rest of that please.

Bob: *"Whether there be knowledge, it shall vanish away. For we know in part, and we prophesy in part. But when that which is perfect is come, then that which is in part shall be done away."*

Ron: *Read verse twelve.*

Bob: *"For now we see through a glass, darkly; but then face to face: now I know in part; but then*

101

shall I know even as also I am known."

Ron: *Has that time come yet? Do we see face to face with Christ? Do you know all things now? NO! People tried to tell me that, that which was perfect was the Bible, yet we don't see face to face. Certainly the perfect One is coming and I want to be ready to meet Him when He does. Don't you?*

Bob: *Yes, sir.*

Ron: *Another area of the Bible that is taken out of context is this verse that you quoted. I Corinthians 14:19: "In the church I had rather speak five words with my understanding, that by my voice I might teach others also, than ten thousand words in an unknown tongue." You know there is a very large church group that conducts their service in Latin and no one can understand them.*

I can honestly say I have never heard anyone preach in tongues in my church. Yet I have seen tongues used by the Lord, in a beautiful way, to back up what the preacher had just said. It's like a telegram from heaven. It lets us know the Lord knows where we are, what we are doing, and what we need. He cares so much that He takes a little time out from His busy schedule and sends us a special message. I really do appreciate a personal Savior like that. Do you have this in your church?

Bob: *No . . . no we don't Ron.*

Ron: *One verse people very seldom quote by Brother Paul is the one just before nineteen. Read verse eighteen please.*

102

Bob: *"I thank my God, I speak with tongues more than ye all."*

Ron: *Do you see now how Paul was misquoted about speaking in tongues?*

Bob: *Yes, I sure do.*

Ron: *Another misquoted statement about tongues is people say that he that prophesieth is greater than he that speaks in tongues. They leave out one important word. The word <u>except</u>: "except he interprets, that the church may receive edifying."*

Another time when Christians speak in tongues is in their private prayers to God. Read I Corinthians 14:2.

Bob: *"For he that speaketh in an unknown tongue speaketh not unto men, but unto God: for no man understandeth him; howbeit in the spirit he speaketh mysteries."*

Ron: *Bob, in review God uses speaking in tongues in at least four different situations.*

One, when you receive the gift of the Holy Ghost you will speak in tongues. Another is the gift of tongues that is used in the church to edify the service. Another is the private prayer to God that we just read about. And another example is singing in tongues in I Corinthians 14:14-15.

I do not have the gift of tongues, but I do have the gift of the Holy Ghost.

Bob: *Ron, I am afraid I might get the wrong spirit if I start trying to speak in tongues.*

Ron: *God will not allow that to happen. He knows our heart and He has more power than any other spirit. Please read Luke 11:9-13; Jesus is talking there.*

Bob: *"And I say unto you, Ask, and it shall be given you; seek, and ye shall find; knock, and it shall be opened unto you. For every one that asketh receiveth; and he that seeketh findeth; and to him that knocketh it shall be opened. If a son shall ask bread of any of you that is a father, will he give him a stone? or if he ask a fish, will he for a fish give him a serpent? Or if he shall ask an egg, will he offer him a scorpion? If ye then, being evil, know how to give good gifts unto your children: how much more shall your heavenly Father give the Holy Spirit to them that ask him?"*

Ron: *That's very plain isn't it, Bob?*

Bob: *It sure is.*

Ron: *Bob, God has now led you to a place in truth like He did Cornelius. It's up to you what you do with this truth. I believe you are a very sincere man like Cornelius was, so much so that God allowed me to show you some things in the Scriptures, like Peter spoke to Cornelius. According to the Bible Cornelius was not saved even though he was a devout man, prayed to God always and gave much alms to the people. We find in Acts 11:14 the account where the following was said, "Who shall tell thee words, whereby thou and all thy house shall be saved." Those same words are true today.*

"Repent, and be baptized every one of you in the name of Jesus Christ for the remission of sins, and ye shall receive the gift of the Holy Ghost" (Acts 2:38).

The only people that I have ever heard preach and teach against this great truth are the ones

104

who have not obeyed it.

Yes, the Holy Ghost is for us today. Thousands are receiving it every week worldwide. He is truly pouring out His Spirit upon all flesh. As is stated in the Bible, God will give the Holy Ghost to them that obey Him.

Bob: *Ron, I want the Spirit. I want to be baptized in Jesus' name. I want to do what God wants me to do. Not only for me, Ron, but for my family as well. I want to be able to teach others as you have taught me.*

Ron: *Bob, if you will remember our discussion in the beginning we asked God to open our hearts that we might understand the Scriptures in a very simple prayer. That's one prayer God will always answer if we will let Him. All I have been is a guide today to show you where to find God's truth. Now it's up to you.*

Bob: *Let's call your pastor to see when I can get baptized. Do you think he will have time to baptize me after church tonight?*

Ron: *He will love to do that tonight. Not only will he be awaiting this great event, Jesus says in Luke 15:10 that there will be joy in the presence of the angels of God over this wonderful accomplishment. So when you come up out of that water tonight, I want you to forget about everything except this scene in the grandstands of heaven. Raise your hands to Jesus and tell Him how wonderful He is, with your voice. He will fill you with the Holy Ghost and begin to speak through you in that heavenly language unknown to you.*

105

I have seen many men like Bob come to that point. Some receive the Holy Ghost during song service, some receive the Spirit when praying at the altar, some receive the Spirit when baptized and some delay until weeks later. But they all are very grateful because someone explained the Word of God to them.

How many Bobs, or Marys, or friends or neighbors do you know that do not have this wonderful experience?

If you do not feel confident as yet to lead them through the Scriptures, let them read this account. That's the reason I wrote out all Scriptures used. To make it easy for you and them to flow through God's Word.

God bless you in this great work of witnessing.

chapter nine

FINANCIAL PLANNING FOR CHRISTIANS

You may ask, what has financial planning got to do with witnessing? I say a lot, if your financial planning is in accordance to the Word of God. One of the ways I am able to lead the conversation to Jesus, with the world, is by showing them what He has done for me. Money gets people's attention in a hurry. Money talks.

I want to make one point loud and clear. That is, when I came to Jesus I had nothing but a large amount of debts. Everything that I now have is a blessing from God. I cannot take credit for any of the financial blessings that God has sent my way. I only try to obey His investment plan and He does the rest.

Have you ever thought of the commission or percentage that God gives? That's right, He pays 90%; He only asks for 10%. Most realtors I know work for 6%. God pays me 90%.

Let me explain! There are good deals and investments that come my way that I know not of. God sends them my way because He knows that I will put a large part of my earnings back into His work. No, He doesn't need me because He owns the world and all things that are in the world. I need Him. Of course, the devil is quick to say that I only give to get something in return. We'll cover that lie later.

Please know that I am not bragging, not about myself, but about my God. God wants you to prosper. He has given us so many promises in His Book that "if we will, He will." When you read the following accounts I want you to know and understand that I give God the credit. I also want you to know that it is hard for me to expose myself in this matter for fear of being misunderstood. Money doesn't mean anything to me, yet God wants you and me to prosper. He said that we should prosper as our soul prospereth. (See I Kings 2:3; III John 2.) God wants you to know and practice His financial plan so He can bless you. There is as much truth in this as there is in the plan of salvation. Both plans were written by the same God.

When I came to Jesus I had very little and in a very short time I had nothing at all. I thought this new life is not really what I expected it to be. Then I found the words of Jesus in Matthew. Matthew 19:29 says, "And every one that hath forsaken houses, or brethren, or sisters, or father, or mother, or wife, or children, or lands for my name's sake, shall receive an *hundredfold,* and shall inherit everlasting life." I had a promise that if I gave up things or people for His *name's sake* then He would bless me. I am sure that you too had to give up some of the above for His name's sake; not for His titles, Father, Son, and Holy Ghost. That was the beginning of the exchange principle of God. "If you will, I will." I ask pastors to forgive me for writing on this subject, for I know that this is taught from the pulpit. I also know that pastors sometimes hold back on this very important subject for fear of being misunderstood. So let me tell the laymen from a layman's point of view how God will bless them and in return bless the church.

I want to make my laymen brethren a little upset at themselves and change their attitude about this important plan of God so they too can be blessed. I also know that most of our laymen are giving as they should. This is for the ones that are holding back just a little because they might not fully understand what they are missing. They might have been absent the day that the sermon was preached on this subject.

Let's review the Word of God together on financial planning. Mark 12:42-44 says, "And there came a certain poor widow, and she threw in two mites . . . And he called unto him his disciples, and saith unto them, Verily I say unto you, That this poor widow hath cast more in, than all . . . For all they did cast in of their abundance; but she of her want did cast in all that she had, even all her living." Jesus looked at the amount the people gave. This is known as sacrificial giving—doing without temporal things temporarily in order to secure eternal benefits.

> *"Every man according as he purposeth in his heart, so let him give, not grudgingly, or of necessity: for God loveth a cheerful giver"* (II Corinthians 9:7).

Now let's look at the great lie with which the devil impresses us: that it is selfish and wrong to expect something in return when we give to God's work. Remember that Satan was in a favored position in heaven and got fired because he misrepresented the truth. Here again he is misrepresenting the facts.

The entire twenty-eighth chapter of Deuteronomy tells of the many blessings of God, if we are obedient. Verse eight says, "The LORD shall command the blessing upon thee in thy storehouses, and in all that thou settest thine hand unto; and he shall bless thee in the land." Our relationship is based on the exchange principle.

Is it wrong to want something for yourself? No. You want salvation, health, peace and success. This is not selfishness. Selfishness is when you want something at the expense of others. Is it wrong to expect financial blessings when you give to God's work? No. Jesus gave it for motivation. Luke 6:38 says, "Give, and it shall be given unto you; good measure, pressed down, and shaken together, and running over, shall men give into your bosom." It's like planting a grain of corn in the field. You plant expecting it to grow. Your release determines your increase.

Money represents you. What you do with money represents your attitude. It can be a very dangerous product of your work and toil or it can be a blessing to you and the work of God. It can produce greed or it can help in the time of need. Giving is God's cure for greed. Giving impresses God.

> "Honour the LORD with thy substance, and with the firstfruits of all thine increase: so shall thy barns be filled with plenty, and thy presses shall burst out with new wine" (Proverbs 3:9-10).

Giving is a public declaration that you have faith in God. An offering reveals a confident heart, a faithful heart, a thankful heart, a generous heart. You tell your loved ones that you care for them by providing for their financial needs. You tell God that you love Him by providing for His earthly ministries' financial needs. When you release your money to God this shows that your money does not control you; you control your money.

"Man cannot out-give God. God will be indebted to no man." "Offerings to God are seeds planted in holy soil" are some beautiful principles I have heard on giving.

How does all this tie in with witnessing? I thought you would never ask. In my office I have twenty-two pictures of foreign missionaries that we support monthly. I know very few of these fine families personally. Yet, I know that they are doing the work of the Lord. Therefore I team up with them in this effort.

When businessmen or customers come into my office, they see these plaques displayed and these really get their attention. They are surprised when I explain that these are not my achievements, but these are my "partners in missions." "What's that?" they usually ask. Then I get to witness to them about God. "How can you support so many?" they usually ask. It's easy to tell them on the exchange plan, and the financial plan of God. I gave God my sins and He gave me forgiveness; I gave Him a troubled heart and He gave me a new heart; I give Him tithes and offerings and He releases financial blessings. It's the principle of total prosperity. This shows them that God is in control. They usually want to know more about God.

I will now share with you a few blessings that God has given me through the exchange principle. Please don't get the wrong idea. I give God the glory. I also give back to

111

Him a lot more than 10%; I owe the first 10%, anything after that is a gift.

Shortly after I turned my life over to Jesus, a brother in one of our Louisiana churches told me about an oil and gas deal in his area. This oil field was depleted and the surface equipment was to be sold to the highest bidder. He said that there might be a little gas remaining that could be produced before selling the equipment. After much praying about this venture, we decided to bid on the project. We made a promise to God that if we got this project we would give the first $25,000 profit to His work. We thought that there would only be about that much profit, and the entire operation would be over in a few weeks. The local geologist and oil companies said that there was nothing there and they had all the charts to prove their points.

The old devil kept trying to stop us in every way possible. The only thing we had going for us was faith in God, which is all we needed. The Lord gave my partner this verse:

"And I will rebuke the devourer for your sakes, and he shall not destroy the fruits of your ground" (Malachi 3:11).

We got the bid on the project, although we bid against some large oil companies. We started producing the four oil and gas wells on the 640 acres lease thinking it would last only a few days. We kept our promise about the $25,000. That was seven long years ago and that gas field is still producing. The geologist cannot understand it. They say there is no gas there. Neither was any meal left in the widow's barrel yet it continued to produce. That oil field has produced over $2 million and is still producing. We continue to support the work of God from those earnings and He has supported us. The same can happen to you.

I had never sold a car in my life. Shortly after I got in the church I had an idea about selling Mercedes-Benz automobiles for European delivery in Stuttgart, Germany. Again my wife and I agreed to put a large amount of those profits into the work of the Lord. The first year was slow, the second year increased, the third year sales really grew and by the fourth year we were the largest selling group of this type in the United States. We give God all the glory.

I started in the real estate business with the same commitment. My twin brother and my partner in the oil and gas business joined me in this venture. We are now the largest developers on a large resort lake. God has really blessed us. Why? The exchange principle. God has allowed me to own three corporations and five other businesses. Remember when I came to Him, I had nothing.

Is this a good witness? It allows me to be in the presence of bankers, lawyers, and financial men from all walks of life. They too want to hear about something that can give them peace within. They have souls that need saving. Just this week a lawyer friend of mine whose wife is getting a master's degree in divinity said that they had never heard the account of the Holy Spirit in the Book of Acts. I hope to get a Home Bible Study with them soon.

I have seen God do miracles for others as well when they put the exchange principle to work as I know you have. No, I do not seek money or riches. I seek the will and plan of God; then He gives me the riches with a peaceful heart. Not wealth such as Elvis Presley, Howard Hughes, or others had that was a curse to them. "If you will, He will." Remember it's not how much you give that counts; it's how much you hold back that God looks at.

Only the devil and the IRS find this principle hard to accept. I have gotten to witness to a few IRS agents because of my giving. They have souls too. The best investment you'll ever make or can ever make is investing into the work of God. This gives man an opportunity to be a limited partner with God. This is better than any hot tip from your stockbroker. Not only will you receive blessings in this life. They will continue to pay off in the next life when you invest with God. The retirement plan is beyond human thinking.

Not long ago one of our church members died after a long battle with cancer. I was impressed to give this family $2,000 to cover the funeral expenses. When my pastor delivered the money to the widow, she began to cry. She told the pastor that she didn't know how she was going to pay for the funeral until he came with the money. She had been quoted a price of exactly $2,000 which she didn't have. God didn't need to give that money back. But He did, many times over. Don't be afraid to help your brother or sister through the church. Always talk this over with your pastor first.

William Colgate left home at the age of sixteen with nothing more than the clothes on his back because his family was too poor to support him. He met an old man on his journey and asked him for advice. The old man prayed with young William and told him to make an honest living and pay the Lord all that belongs to Him of every dollar he earned.

William practiced giving to God as the old man advised. He soon went from a hired hand in the soap factory to a partner. After the partner died William became sole owner of the business. He started giving one tenth of his earnings to the Lord, then 20 percent, then 30 percent, then 40 percent and finally 50 percent. He prospered more than ever. He gave millions to the work of the Lord and left a name that will never die.

PART II

chapter ten

RIGHTLY DIVIDING THE WORD OF TRUTH

We all know the plan of salvation. But do we know how to show others and prove to ourselves what the plan is? When I first got into the church the only Scripture I knew was Acts 2:38. I thought I could take on the whole world with just that one verse. Not so.

I would talk with people of other beliefs and they would put me in the corner very fast with their knowledge of the Bible. They would quote Scriptures like Romans 10:9: "That if thou shalt confess with thy mouth the Lord Jesus, and shalt believe in thine heart that God hath raised him from the dead, thou shalt be saved." They would say all you have to do is to confess Christ and you are saved. So here I was full of the Holy Ghost, baptized in Jesus' name but could not defend my salvation. Not only was I embarrassed, I was also ashamed before God that I could not defend my belief. I had laid my soul on the line for all of eternity for my belief yet I could not define it.

Let's look at the Bible and see what it really says about this very important subject.

First of all we must rightly divide the word of truth. Look at Matthew, Mark, Luke, and John for example. These books of the New Testament are history about the birth, ministry, death, and resurrection of Jesus Christ. Jesus' plan for us had not been laid down at this period of time. He was getting the world ready to receive His plan in His testament. When did Jesus' last will and testament become effective? When He died. The same way your last will and testament becomes effective. You must die; otherwise it is useless. Hebrews 9:16-17 says:

> *"For where a testament is, there must also of necessity be the death of the testator. For a testament is of force after men are dead: otherwise it is of no strength at all while the testator liveth."*

Therefore, Jesus' will for us did not become effective until He died.

He had to die in order to send His Spirit back to dwell within us. While He was on this earth He could only be with a local assembly at one time. Now He can be with everyone throughout the whole world at the same time. Jesus said, "It is expedient for you that I go away: for if I go not away, the Comforter will not come unto you; but if I depart, I will send him unto you" (John 16:7).

It's sad to hear people say all you have to do is believe on the Lord Jesus Christ and you are saved. He died in vain for those people. People believed on Him before He died. The Bible even says the devils believe on Him and tremble. Are they saved?

No, friend, He had to shed His precious blood for us to be redeemed. Acts 20:28 says,

"Take heed therefore unto yourselves, and to all the flock, over the which the Holy Ghost hath made you overseers, to feed the church of God, which he hath purchased with his own blood."

Our plan of salvation was not put into effect until the Day of Pentecost in the Book of Acts when the Lord sent His Spirit to dwell in man. Most denominations will agree that the church was born in the Book of Acts. The remainder of the books in the New Testament are letters written back to the established church with the exception of Revelation which is prophecy.

Therefore, we go to the Book of Acts for the plan of salvation—not in the history books of Matthew, Mark, Luke, and John or in the Epistles or letters written to the church. However, all these books point ahead to or refer back to the plan of salvation that was established on the Day of Pentecost.

For example, let's examine the great commissions that Jesus gave and see if they are in order with Acts 2:38.

The Great Commissions

Matthew 28:19: *"Go ye therefore, and teach all nations, baptizing them in the name of the Father, and of the Son, and of the Holy Ghost."* *[Teaching them!]*

Mark 16:15-17: *"Go ye into all the world, and preach the gospel to every creature. He that believeth and is baptized shall be saved; but he that believeth not shall be damned. And these* *signs shall follow them that believe; In my name shall they cast out devils; they shall speak with new tongues."*

Luke 24:47-49: *"And that repentance and remission of sins should be preached in his name among all nations, beginning at Jerusalem . . . And, behold, I send the promise of my Father upon you: but tarry ye in the city of Jerusalem, until ye be endued with power from on high."*

John 20:22-23: *"He breathed on them, and saith unto them, Receive ye the Holy Ghost: whose soever sins ye remit, they are remitted unto them; and whose soever sins ye retain, they are retained."*

Let's look at how all these great commissions tie in with Acts 2:38. Consider:

Matthew 28:19 He told them to baptize in the name. Peter obeyed this command when he said to be baptized in the name of Jesus.

Mark 16:15-17 Says also to be baptized and the sign of tongues would be present. They were.

Luke 24:47-49 Says that repentance and remission of sins should be preached, and they should receive power. Peter preached repent and be baptized for the remission of sins and they received the power of the Holy Ghost.

John 20:22-23 Receive ye the Holy Ghost. They did, all 3,120 of them in one day. Also note that He said whose soever sins ye remit, they are remitted and whose soever sins ye retain they are retained.

How can men remit or retain sins? What is the first thing that a minister will ask a candidate for baptism? Have you repented of your sins? If he has not then the minister will not baptize him, thus retaining his sins, or if he has repented he will baptize him remitting his sins.

The sum total of the great commission in Matthew, Mark, Luke, and John that Jesus gave is to repent and be baptized in the name of Jesus Christ for the remission of sins and receive the gift of the Holy Ghost.

Don't let people drag you over into the history books of Matthew, Mark, Luke, and John or into the Epistles written to the established church for the plan of salvation.

The Bible says:

"Study to shew thyself approved unto God, a workman that needeth not to be ashamed, rightly dividing the word of truth" (II Timothy 2:15).

chapter eleven

QUESTIONS AND/OR DOCTRINES TO OVERCOME

First of all, let me say that it is not our place to judge anyone. Let the Word do that. Never let the candidate get by with saying these familiar words: "Well, if what you say is true then all these other people are lost." Be quick to respond to this statement with, "That it is not my words. I am only reading them from the Bible." Otherwise he will say that you are judging him. Hand him the Bible and let him read the plan of salvation himself. Then the question is between him and God. I always tell my candidates not to take my word for anything, nor my pastor's word, but take the Word of God and then if he still has questions ask him to ask God to open his heart to understand the Scriptures.

The reason that most people are deceived today is that they do not know what is in the Bible. They have been sitting back and taking someone else's word on what the Bible says.

I know this to be true because this is exactly what I did, and so have many others. I was lazy enough to let some far-out group tell me thus and so. I accepted what they said because they seemed to be sincere and nice people.

The Bible challenges us to "Search the scriptures; for in them ye think ye have eternal life" (John 5:39). It also warns us in II Timothy 3:7 about men who will be "ever learning, and never able to come to the knowledge of the truth."

One of the things that puzzled me most was how people could preach and teach something diametrically opposed to God's will and way. How could men preach from the pulpit from the same Bible that I had, yet come up with something completely different from the plan of salvation as recorded in Acts 2:38? There were sincere people in these churches, yet they did not measure up with what the Bible said. I asked the Lord to show me what this was. He answered by His words:

> "And with all deceivableness of unrighteousness in them that perish; because they received not the love of the truth, that they might be saved. And for this cause God shall send them strong delusion, that they should believe a lie: That they all might be damned who believed not the truth, but had pleasure in unrighteousness" (II Thessalonians 2:10).

I had to say, "Thank you Jesus for answering my prayer." He let me see quickly that people who reject His Word would be allowed to believe anything. That's the reason we have over 1800 different religious groups in the world. Are these great numbers right? Ephesians 4:5 says that there is only "One Lord, one faith, one baptism" not 1800 different brands.

Then I questioned, "Lord, what about the ones that believe in receiving the Holy Spirit and have great miracles in their churches? Yet, they don't have a holiness standard nor do they baptize in Jesus' name." I have even seen these things performed before my own eyes. In fact, I was with a group like this when I received the Holy Ghost. I was very confused!

Praise the Lord, He answered my prayer again with His Word. He directed me to:

"Not every one that saith unto me, Lord, Lord, shall enter into the kingdom of heaven; but he that doeth the will of my Father which is in heaven. Many will say to me in that day, Lord, Lord, have we not prophesied in thy name? and in thy name have cast out devils? and in thy name done many wonderful works? And then will I profess unto them, I never knew you: depart from me, ye that work iniquity" (Matthew 7:21-23).

Talk about getting my attention, the above Scripture did, especially the twenty-third verse. Those poor people on that great day will be cast away from the Lord, yet all the while they thought they were right.

"Lord, don't let me be deceived," was my prayer. "Open my understanding that I might understand the Scriptures (Luke 24:25). Thank you for the revelation of the truth."

I still had questions about this group because I

127

received the Holy Ghost there and saw many others also receive this gift. (I also saw many taught how to speak in tongues by "repeat after me" type instructions which I knew was error.)

Again the Lord directed me to His Word and showed me that men could receive the Holy Ghost anywhere. The surroundings didn't matter. What mattered was the condition of the heart and the hunger for God. Then He showed me the purpose of the Holy Ghost as a teacher.

"He shall teach you all things" (John 14:26).
"Howbeit when he, the Spirit of truth, is come,
he will guide you into all truth" (John 16:13).

Therefore the Holy Ghost led me to the truth, and since there is no respecter of persons with God, I am sure He will also lead others to the truth. When I saw the truth, I had to depart from the group that I was with.

That reminds me of the story about the rat poison. You can take 95% good hamburger meat and mix 5% rat poison with it and kill every rat in Texas. Why is this so? Because you have enough of the good stuff to fool the rat, yet enough poison to kill him. The same can be done with God's truth. You can take 95% truth and mix 5% error with it and destroy every so-called Christian around. The devil doesn't care how much of the good stuff you get just as long as he has enough control of the group to inject enough error or poison to kill. Again let's refer to Matthew 7:21. These people had the power of truth yet they had the error or poison on that last day. Look how the Lord reprimanded the churches in Revelation. They had done a few good things yet they had error or poison in their groups.

chapter twelve

BELIEF, WORKS, AND FAITH

The first time that I went to an altar asking God to forgive me I was confronted with the question of works, faith, and believing.

Shortly after I went to the altar a minister came and knelt down beside me. He had a small New Testament in his hand and opened it to Romans 10:9. He read that verse of Scripture to me and asked if I thought the Bible was the true word of God. Of course I said yes. Then he said, "You are saved." He assured me that I was saved and that the saving knowledge would come by faith. I couldn't get anymore saved than I just was by his assuring words.

But I felt so empty. I was also very puzzled because I believed what he had read before I went to church. Yet who was I to question this man? If that was all there was to being saved, then why bother with going to church, paying tithes, and other such duties?

I had come to a time and place in my life that I realized that only God had the answers. I began to think about eternity and compare it with the present life. How foolish I had been, trusting in myself to get me through this life. What would I have to offer God on that great day? Nothing but a pack of sins. I wanted to rid myself of those sins before stepping out into eternity, before facing God with my rebellious life.

The one thing that I didn't want was religion. There are many religious orders on this earth, and according to the Bible most of them are wrong (Hinduism is a religion; worshiping the stars is a religion). I wanted salvation. The word *salvation* means preservation from destruction. Only God has that plan. He has it all written out in His Book. Yet man is only taking out bits and pieces of that Book and making their own doctrine. The Bible tells us about them:

> *"Having a form of godliness, but denying the power thereof: from such turn away . . . Ever learning, and never able to come to the knowledge of the truth" (II Timothy 3:5-7).*
>
> *"But in vain they do worship me, teaching for doctrines the commandments of men" (Matthew 15:9).*

I didn't want the commandments of men. I wanted the plan of God. The Lord had spared my life so many times. As a fighter pilot in the Navy, I lost over 200 of my closest friends flying the same type of aircraft and the same type of mission that I was flying.

Today, I should be dead and in hell because I was no better than these pilots. Yet because of the mercy of God, not of my own skill, I survived. I don't know why! But somehow God had mercy on me. That's the reason I want to do His will and not the will of men. That's the reason that I take time to witness to others because I am living on borrowed time. That's the reason it really concerns me to see people being led to a half truth whose "end thereof is death."

No, I don't want to play church. No, I don't want to be a part of the great social club of the religious community. No, I don't want the preacher to pat me on the back and say you are really doing well when we both know better. No, I don't want the doctrine of "once saved always saved" and end up in hell. No, I don't want to be elevated to some high office or position in the church because of my financial statement. No, I don't want to be misled. I want the truth. I want salvation.

Let's look at the verse of Scripture that the minister read me that night. This is the Scripture that he and thousands of others are placing their soul's salvation on for all eternity. First notice that this Scripture comes from Romans. In other words this was written to the established church or to people who had already received the plan of salvation back on the Day of Pentecost.

> *"That if thou shalt confess with thy mouth the Lord Jesus, and shalt believe in thine heart that God hath raised him from the dead, thou shalt be saved" (Romans 10:9).*

If there was a verse ever taken out of context, this was it. That's like pulling out the one verse that says "Jesus wept" and believe that for thirty-three years all He did was "bawl and squall." Yet we know that there is much more to the plan of salvation than mentally believing. The Bible says:

131

> *"Thou believest that there is one God; thou doest well: the devils also believe, and tremble" (James 2:19).*

So if mental belief is all that is necessary for salvation then the devils are saved. Mental acknowledgement is the first step.

Continue to read the tenth chapter of Romans and see if there is more to the question.

> *"For with the heart man believeth unto right-eousness; and with the mouth confession is made unto salvation. For whosoever shall call upon the name of the Lord shall be saved. [Many churches are built on this one Scripture; I have heard people call on the name of the Lord in vain, are they saved?] How then shall they call on him in whom they have not believed? and how shall they believe in him of whom they have not heard? and how shall they hear without a preacher? And how shall they preach, except they be sent? as it is writ-ten, How beautiful are the feet of them that preach the gospel of peace, and bring glad tidings of good things! But they have not all obeyed the gospel. For Esaias saith, Lord, who hath believed our report? So then faith cometh by hearing, and hear-ing by the word of God" (Romans 10:10, 13-17).*

Verses 14 through 17 really put the question up front on the salvation matter. Look closely at verse 14. "How shall they hear without a preacher?" Verse 15 asks, "How shall they preach, except they be sent." Verse 16 says,

132

"But they have not all obeyed the gospel." Verse 17 says, "So then faith cometh by hearing, and hearing by the word of God."

No, I was not saved that night the so-called (unsent) preacher read me that verse of Scripture. The Bible says that for me to have faith I must *hear* and *obey* the Word of God. I only heard part of the Word of God. The devil believes in God, yet he is not saved. Therefore, the complete Word of God is the saving word, not a part taken out of context.

Let's see what the Bible says about them that believe. Jesus said:

> *"He that believeth on me, as the scripture hath said, out of his belly shall flow rivers of living water. (But this spake he of the Spirit, which they that believe on him should receive: for the Holy Ghost was not yet given; because that Jesus was not yet glorified)" (John 7:38-39).*

The preacher didn't read me this verse when I was pronounced saved by him. The Bible says that if I believe as the Scriptures hath said that I would receive the Holy Ghost. Yet, that night I didn't receive the Holy Ghost. I'll cover the evidence of the Holy Ghost later.

The Scripture also says:

> *"He that believeth and is baptized shall be saved; . . . And these signs shall follow them that believe; in my name shall they cast out devils; they shall speak with new tongues" (Mark 16:16-17).*

133

Well, I failed on two points in that Scripture so I was not saved that night. I was not baptized (I'll cover that commandment later), nor did I speak with new tongues. Yet the Bible plainly says these are the signs of a true believer.

Let's look at an example of a man in the Bible that would have put us all to shame with his devotion. This man could have been a deacon or a board member in just about any church today. Look at Acts 10. Here we find Cornelius. The Bible says he was a "devout man, and one that feared God with all his house, which gave much alms to the people, and prayed to God alway," yet according to the Bible he was not saved until he had completed God's plan of salvation. Look at Acts 10:33. God had some other commandments for him. Look at verses 44-48. Just like Jesus said back in Mark 16:16.

When Cornelius obeyed the Lord, he received the Holy Ghost and spoke with tongues and was baptized in Jesus' name. Was he saved prior to this? Again let's go to the Bible for the answer. Peter answers this question in Acts 11:14 when he recounts the word of Cornelius: "Who shall tell thee words, whereby thou and all thy house shall be saved." So according to the Bible Cornelius was not saved even though he prayed to God always until he heard the Word (Acts 10:44) and acted upon the Word in the forty-fifth and forty-eighth verses.

You don't have to judge people. Let the Word of God judge them. Do they measure up to what this devout man had to do to be saved, or don't they?

The next big point the people made was, "You are not saved by works but by faith." "You can't get good enough to get saved." "Jesus Christ plus nothing saved you."

"Baptism is works" and so on. Again let's go to the Word of God for these answers.

The favorite Scripture that is used to prove the fact that man does not have to do one thing, or cannot do one thing to be saved is Ephesians 2:5: "By grace ye are saved." Look at Ephesians 2:8-9, "For by grace are ye saved through faith; and that not of yourselves: it is the gift of God: not of works, lest any man should boast." Let's look at the New International Version of the Bible. Ephesians 2:5, "It is by grace you have been saved." Verse 8 says, "For it is by grace you have been saved, through faith—and this not from your selves, it is the gift of God." Verse 9 says, "Not by works, so that no one can boast."

We all know that we cannot save ourselves. Only Jesus Christ can save us. But the Bible plainly says that we must apply what He has done for us, else it is of no effect. Titus 2:11 says, "For the grace of God that bringeth salvation hath appeared to all men." Are all men saved? The Bible says that few are saved. The Bible says in Philippians 2:12 to "Work out your own salvation with fear and trembling."

Again in Ephesians it tells us of the work or struggle to be accomplished.

"Finally, my brethren, be strong in the Lord, and in the power of his might. Put on the whole armour of God, that ye may be able to stand against the wiles of the devil. For we wrestle not against flesh and blood, but against principalities, against powers, against the rulers of the darkness of this world, against spiritual wickedness in high places. Wherefore take unto you the

135

whole armour of God, that ye may be able to withstand in the evil day, and having done all, to stand. Stand therefore, having your loins girt about with truth, and having on the breastplate of righteousness; and your feet shod with the preparation of the gospel of peace; above all, taking the shield of faith, wherewith ye shall be able to quench all the fiery darts of the wicked. And take the helmet of salvation, and the sword of the Spirit, which is the word of God: praying always with all prayer and supplication in the Spirit, and watching thereunto with all persever-ance and supplication for all saints" (Ephesians 6:10-18).

Please reread the above verses of Scripture and then tell me that is not work. Another good example of faith and works is found in the book of James:

"What doth it profit, my brethren, though a man say he hath faith, and have not works? can faith save him? . . . Even so faith, if it hath not works, is dead, being alone. Yea, a man may say, Thou hast faith, and I have works: shew me thy faith without thy works, and I will shew thee my faith by my works. Thou believest that there is one God; thou doest well: the devils also believe, and tremble. But wilt thou know, O vain man, that faith without works is dead? . . . Seest thou how faith wrought with his works, and by works was faith made perfect? . . . Ye see then how that by works a man is justified, and not by

136

faith only . . . For as the body without the spirit is dead, so faith without works is dead also" (James 2:14-26).

The Book of Revelation tells also that people will be judged by their works. How can Jesus say "Well done" when you haven't done well?

Peter believed on Jesus before the crucifixion, yet according to the Bible he was not converted at that time. Jesus said to him in Luke 22:32, "When thou art converted." When did this conversion take place? Read Acts 2:38 for the answer.

chapter thirteen

ETERNAL SECURITY – FACT OR FICTION?

The first record of eternal security being taught in the Bible is the account of Eve and the serpent in the Garden of Eden. The serpent told Eve to go ahead and disobey God's commandments: "Ye shall not surely die," but that day Adam and Eve died spiritually. Genesis gives us the whole story.

The *New International Version* says it as follows: "Now the serpent was more crafty." Today we have crafty men in religious authority who are telling their members that once saved always saved; no matter what they do, say, or think they will not die or be separated from God spiritually.

Let's find out what the Bible says about this subject. There are so many verses of Scripture that are against eternal security as it is being taught today that I will not be able to show them all, but will list enough to show that there is no truth in this doctrine.

"Brethren, if any of you do err from the truth,

and one convert him; let him know, that he which converteth the sinner from the error of his way shall save a soul from death, and shall hide a multitude of sins" (James 5:19-20).

Note that James is talking about a *brother* in Christ who has sin charged against him. He says his soul will die if no one converts the sinner. What is the death of a soul? Separation from God. Is this brother eternally secure? No.

"Many will follow their shameful ways and will bring the way of truth into disrepute. In their greed these teachers will exploit you with stories they have made up. Their condemnation has long been hanging over them, and their destruction has not been sleeping. For if God did not spare angels when they sinned, but sent them to hell, putting them into gloomy dungeons to be held for judgment; if he did not spare the ancient world when he brought the flood on its ungodly people, but protected Noah, a preacher of righteousness, and seven others; if he condemned the cities of Sodom and Gomorrah by burning them to ashes, and made them an example of what is going to happen to the ungodly; . . . This is especially true of those who follow the corrupt desire of the sinful nature and despise authority . . . with eyes full of adultery, they never stop sinning; . . . They have left the straight way . . . who loved the wages of wickedness. . . . Blackest darkness is reserved for them. . . . If they have escaped the corruption of the world by knowing our Lord and

*Savior Jesus Christ and are again entangled in it,
and overcome, they are worse off at the end than
they were at the beginning. . . . Of them the
proverbs are true: 'A dog returns to its vomit,' and,
'A sow that is washed goes back to her wallow-
ing in the mud'" (II Peter 2:2-22 NIV).*

How plain can the Scriptures be? The latter end is
worse than the beginning. They were lost in the beginning. What hope do they have in the latter end? None!
Listen to what Jesus says:

*"Those on the rock are the ones who receive
the word with joy when they hear it, but they
have no root. They believe for a while, but in the
time of testing they fall away" (Luke 8:13 NIV).*

Here Jesus is talking about persons who are believers
for a while, yet during time of testing, they fall away.

*"But he that shall endure unto the end, the
same shall be saved" (Matthew 24:13 KJV).*
*"Whosoever transgresseth, and abideth not
in the doctrine of Christ, hath not God" (II John 9
KJV).*
*"Anyone who runs ahead and does not con-
tinue in the teaching of Christ does not have
God" (II John 9 NIV).*

How plain can it be? Can you have eternal security
without God?
Again the Bible says:

141

> *"He who overcomes will, like them, be dressed in white. I will never blot his name from the book of life" (Revelation 3:5 NIV).*

Who is going to be dressed in white? He that overcomes. What happens to the ones who do not overcome? His name will be erased from the book of life. Does that sound like eternal security?

Jesus says:

> *"Be careful, or your hearts will be weighed down with dissipation, drunkenness and the anxieties of life, and that day will close on you unexpectedly like a trap. . . . Be always on the watch, and pray that you may be able to escape all that is about to happen, and that you may be able to stand before the Son of Man" (Luke 21:34, 36 NIV).*

Here Jesus warns His people to watch and pray that they might be worthy. He does not say to go ahead and sin a little every day and I'll over look it. He warns us that we could be caught in the trap at anytime so we had better be ready.

> *"And if the righteous scarcely be saved, where shall the ungodly and the sinner appear?" (I Peter 4:18).*
> *"Follow peace with all men, and holiness, without which no man shall see the Lord" (Hebrews 12:14).*

I don't think this needs an explanation. It's so simply stated; if you are not holy you will not see God.

"If we claim to have fellowship with him yet walk in darkness, we lie and do not live by the truth. The man who says, 'I know him,' but does not do what he commands is a liar, and the truth is not in him. He who does what is sinful is of the devil, because the devil has been sinning from the beginning . . . No one who is born of God will continue to sin, because God's seed remains in him; he cannot go on sinning, because he has been born of God. This is how we know who the children of God are and who the children of the devil are: Anyone who does not do what is right is not a child of God" (I John 1:6; 2:4; 3:8-10 NIV).

Note how strong this Scripture is. Anyone who does not do right is not of God.

Again Jesus speaks in Matthew:

"Not everyone that saith unto me, Lord, Lord, shall enter into the kingdom of heaven; but he that doeth the will of my Father which is in heaven. Many will say to me in that day, Lord, Lord, have we not prophesied in thy name? and in thy name have cast out devils? and in thy name done many wonderful works? And then will I profess unto them, I never knew you: depart from me, ye that work iniquity" (Matthew 7:21-23).

Jesus is talking about persons who believed in Him. They used His name to perform the mighty acts; however, due to the evil of iniquity they practiced, Jesus told them to depart from Him. Does this sound like eternal security? I should say not.

In the book of John Jesus says:

> "*I am the true vine, and my Father is the husbandman. Every branch in me that beareth not fruit he taketh away: and every branch that beareth fruit, he purgeth it, that it may bring forth more fruit. Now ye are clean through the word which I have spoken unto you. Abide in me, and I in you. As the branch cannot bear fruit of itself, except it abide in the vine; no more can ye, except ye abide in me. I am the vine, ye are the branches: He that abideth in me, and I in him, the same bringeth forth much fruit: for without me ye can do nothing. If a man abide not in me, he is cast forth as a branch, and is withered; and men gather them, and cast them into the fire, and they are burned*" (John 15:1-6).

Jesus says if anyone does not remain in Him, they will be thrown into the fire and burned.

> "*Be imitators of God, therefore, as dearly loved children and live a life of love, just as Christ loved us and gave himself up for us as a fragrant offering and sacrifice to God. But among you there must not be even a hint of sexual immorality, or of any kind of impurity, or of greed, because these are improper for God's holy people. Nor should there be any obscenity, foolish talk or coarse joking, which are out of*

place, but rather thanksgiving. For of this you can be sure: No immoral, impure or greedy person—such a man is an idolator—has any inheritance in the kingdom of Christ and of God" (Ephesians 5:1-5 NIV).

These Scriptures clearly state that such a person described above has no inheritance with God. Would a person like this be eternally secure if he practiced such sins? The Bible says no.

Read the whole sixth chapter of Romans. Pay particular attention to verse fifteen which says, "What then? shall we sin, because we are not under the law, but under grace? God forbid." Verse 23 plainly states that the wages of sin is death.

"He who does what is sinful is of the devil, because the devil has been sinning from the beginning. The reason the Son of God appeared was to destroy the devil's work. No one who is born of God will continue to sin, because God's seed remains in him; he cannot go on sinning, because he has been born of God. This is how we know who the children of God are and who the children of the devil are: Anyone who does not do what is right is not a child of God; nor is anyone who does not love his brother" (I John 3:8-10 NIV).

Next time you see someone doing wrong and maintaining that the eternal security doctrine is true, just open your Bible and show him these Scriptures.

"It is impossible for those who have once been enlightened, who have tasted the heavenly gift, who have shared in the Holy Spirit, who have tasted the goodness of the word of God and the powers of the coming age, if they fall away, to be brought back to repentance, because to their loss they are crucifying the Son of God all over again and subjecting him to public disgrace" (Hebrews 6:4-6 NIV).

The Bible says we can fall away by sin yet it is taught in many churches today that it is impossible to fall away.

Let's now go to the book of Revelation and get the final account of who will be in heaven and who will not be in heaven.

"He that overcometh shall inherit all things; and I will be his God, and he shall be my son" (Revelation 21:7).

"Blessed are they that do his commandments, that they may have right to the tree of life, and may enter in through the gates into the city" (Revelation 22:14).

Note also who will *not* be in heaven:

"But the fearful, and unbelieving, and the abominable, and murderers, and whoremongers, and sorcerers, and idolaters, and all liars, shall have their part in the lake which burneth with fire and brimstone" (Revelation 21:8).

"Without are dogs, and sorcerers, and

146

whoremongers, and murderers, and idolaters, and whosoever loveth and maketh a lie" (Revelation 22:15).

Yes, Jesus has the final say about this eternal security doctrine.

"Let him who does wrong continue to do wrong; let him who is vile continue to be vile; let him who does right continue to do right; and let him who is holy continue to be holy" (Revelation 22:11 NIV).

He says in the next verse,

"Behold, I am coming soon! My reward is with me, and I will give to everyone according to what he has done" (Revelation 22:12 NIV).

Jesus says in Matthew,

"For I tell you that unless your righteousness surpasses that of the Pharisees and the teachers of the law, you will certainly not enter the kingdom of heaven" (Matthew 5:20 NIV).

The one main Scripture that is used by those who believe "once saved always saved" is Romans 8:35.

In summary, eternal security as being taught by a large religious group is not taught in the Bible. This is doctrine of men.

If once saved always saved was a truth then why

bother with going to church, paying tithes, or reading the Bible? You cannot get anymore saved than you already are. You are just wasting your time. Have fun in life, rob a bank, and be comfortable. Crazy, isn't it?

I heard a preacher say once that when you accept Jesus Christ as your personal Savior there is no way you could be lost. In fact he said, "You are just as saved as any angel in heaven." I remembered the Bible account where a large number of the angels were expelled from heaven for sinning against God. (See Isaiah 14:12; Ezekiel 28:11-19; Revelation 12:4).

Let's look at the meaning of the word *saved.* Note that the same word can be used for past, present, or future tense. Example, I was saved, I am saved, or I will be saved. They are all conditional. I was saved from drowning when I was ten years old. That does not mean that I cannot drown today or in the future. It really depends upon my actions when I get around water whether I am saved from drowning.

Jesus saved me from my sins several years ago. I will be saved today and in the future if I watch my steps when around sin. If I jump back into the lake of sin then I will be lost. That is unless I call for God's help for rescue.

I was often read the verse of Scripture in Romans:

> *"Who shall separate us from the love of Christ? shall tribulation, or distress, or persecution, or famine, or nakedness, or peril, or sword? . . . For I am persuaded, that neither death, nor life, nor angels, nor principalities, nor powers, nor things present, nor things to come, nor height, nor depth, nor any other creature, shall be able to*

separate us from the love of God, which is in Christ Jesus our Lord" (Romans 8:35-39).

After these verses were read the minister would say, "See, nothing you do can separate God's love from you." It is true that God never stops loving; God loves all, both sinner and saint. However, a person can reject or walk away from God's love and so lose his salvation. This Scripture does not teach eternal security for a sinner or saint.

Another so-called candy stick for the once saved always saved group is that they claim that God says our righteousnesses are as filthy rags and we can do nothing good in God's eyes. Well, let's go to the Bible and see what it says:

"But we are all as an unclean thing, and all our righteousnesses are as filthy rags; and we all do fade as a leaf; and our iniquities, like the wind, have taken us away. And there is none that calleth upon thy name, that stirreth up himself to take hold of thee: for thou hast hid thy face from us, and hast consumed us, because of our iniquities" (Isaiah 64:6-7).

Here again are the people confessing to God that they have done wrong. They say we are unclean and because of *our* iniquities God has hid His face from us. God will do the same thing today because He cannot look upon sin.

When someone quotes that God says our righteousness is as filthy rags, just read the Book to them. The reason most people are deceived is that they don't read the Bible but take someone else's word for what it says.

I have also been told of the prodigal son. They say, "See, he sinned and yet he was not lost." Look at the fifteenth chapter of Luke. Brother Luke tells the story starting with verse eleven. We all know the story so in order to condense space let's go to verse eighteen. The son says, "I have sinned against heaven, and before thee." In verse twenty-one he says, "I have sinned against heaven, and in thy sight." In verse twenty-four the father says, "My son was dead, and is alive again: he was lost, and is found." The same statement is repeated in verse thirty-two.

Is this an example of eternal security? No. The son had to come back the same way we have to come back to God if we sin against Him, else we would be lost.

Consider the point. What is the difference between the sin of Peter and of Judas? Both of them sinned against Jesus. Peter denied Jesus and Judas sold Him. Both were wrong. Why then did Peter advance so high in God's chain of command that he was given the keys to the kingdom of heaven while Judas died a sinner? The reason, of course, is that Peter came back to Jesus and repented. Judas died in his sins.

It is sad that many sinners feel a false sense of security when churches teach the doctrine of once saved always saved.

chapter fourteen

THE LAST FLIGHT

Not long ago, as I was jogging, the Lord impressed me with the following thought about the urgency of soulwinning. Please allow me to share this thought with you.

As an Airline Captain, I make many announcements to my passengers as to the conditions of our journey, weather enroute and estimated time of arrival. Please follow through with me on the preparations for the final departure from this earth.

"Ladies and Gentlemen, this is your captain speaking. It is my pleasure to welcome you aboard our flight. We are so pleased that you have elected to fly with us today, and we will do everything we can to make this trip comfortable. We should be taxiing for take-off in just a few moments and once we are airborne we are expecting a very smooth flight.

"I have just been notified that there will be a short delay for last-minute passengers. The Master Controller is the only One that really knows the exact time that we will depart and He is in charge of our departure. He doesn't want to leave anyone behind because this is the last flight. However, when that last ticket is bought we will be on our way. There is no need to hang around this place any longer.

"The Master Controller has been advertising this flight for years. He has had it told from the highway and the hedges, from the housetops and the mountainsides. Now the campaign is about over and we are excited about the journey. Yet, He will delay the flight for those last few passengers. He is so compassionate. I read once where He caused the sun to stand still for just one man.

"Don't be alarmed because of all the commotion in the airplane. The flight attendants noticed that some of the passengers have tried to fly with the wrong tickets. Also, some of the passengers that once had valid tickets have lost their tickets due to neglect and other interests. I heard that one man sold his ticket for a Golden Apple, another sold his for the pleasures in his neighborhood. Of course, these people must be removed from the aircraft before the flight begins. It is not my responsibility to check the tickets. I only advise people to have the proper ticket. It has been said that just prior to departure, there would be a great shaking up of the passengers and some would even turn away.

"Again, Ladies and Gentlemen, please accept my apology for the flight being detained here at the gate. The Master Controller said we must wait on the late arrivals and connecting passengers from other denominations. He will not leave one behind that has made proper reservations. He also has said that, 'Once the door is shut, it cannot be opened until we reach our destination.'

"The Master Controller asked me to pass on some words of congratulations and encouragement to you. He said to tell you that He is proud of each of you and that you have done well. He said that He was heartbroken that many names had to be erased from the manifest at the last minute due to the fact the people didn't know the departure was so close at hand and they were just not ready to go. The other destination had to enlarge itself. One man wanted to go on this flight very bad, but just never got around to making the reservations and paying the price. Another individual made reservations, bought the ticket, and then sold it for the pleasures of this world. One fellow got to the gate and noticed that this was a no-smoking, no-drinking flight. He got mad and tore up his ticket saying, 'They can't tell me what I can and cannot do.' Another man had so many possessions down here which took up all his time that he just didn't want to leave them. One lady had too much excess baggage that held her back. She just couldn't turn loose of those worldly things; besides, the dress code for the flight does not allow blue jeans and hot pants!

"The Master Controller noted that some of you made reservations years ago for this flight, some of you have just recently purchased your tickets and some of you who lost your tickets in the past have re-purchased new ones and have gotten your names back on the manifest. He said to tell you that He is proud of everyone on this flight.

"Notice all the ground personnel working around the airplane getting it ready. These are support people. They won't be making the flight. Yes, they work around the plane and even go inside at times, but when the time comes for us to depart they will not be aboard. The Master

Controller utilizes their service and support and He blesses them for it, but since they have not purchased a ticket they cannot go. They know all about the procedures for making the flight and some of their family members might be on board, but they will be left behind. It's sort of like the scaffolding around a house when it is being built. It is very necessary during construction, but once the house is completed, the ugly old scaffolding is torn down and cast into the fire.

"The Master Controller said that the ones who have gone on before us are eagerly awaiting our arrival. He promises the 'Red Carpet' treatment and He has a great marriage supper planned for all.

"Well, folks, it looks like we are finally about to close the door and start our taxi out for takeoff . . . what's that noise I hear? It sounds like people running down the jetway. The jetway is filling up with excited people. These are those last minute passengers the Master Controller was waiting for. They made it just in time. Look at them coming from every direction, their tickets held high. There are some that purchased their tickets from the First United Pentecostal Church of Dallas, St. Louis, Houston, New York, Frankfurt, and Naples, they are coming from everywhere. They want to go, they want to go---. There is Deanna, John, Albert, Georgia, Betty, Paul and <u>others</u>.

"Ladies and Gentlemen, I have never seen such excitement in all my flying. Everyone is jumping up and down in the aisles. The angels in heaven are rejoicing in the presence of the Master Controller. We are going to make it, we are going to make it.

"The *others* that I underlined are the ones that the Master Controller is waiting for. We need to go out into the

154

highways and hedges and the mountainsides and compel them to come in before this flight departs.

"Think of all those *others*. They are all around us. We need to be their special 'Travel Agents' and help them prepare for this final flight."

Suggested books to read:

The Godhead
by Kenneth Reeves

The Great Commission
by Kenneth Reeves

Handbook on Receiving the Holy Ghost
by Fred Kinzie

How to Receive the Holy Ghost
by J. T Pugh

Acts
by Jet Witherspoon

How to Win Friends and Influence People
by Dale Carnegie

Tracts and Booklets:

The Apostles Doctrine
by S. R. Hanby

Wheel of Prophecy
by C. P. Kilgore

60 Questions on the Godhead
by J. F. Solomon

Water Baptism
by David C. Nevins

Why We Baptize in Jesus' Name
by Mrs. T M. Bowen

Unconditional Eternal Security: Fact or Fable?
by J. E. Gray

The Real Truth about Baptism in Jesus' Name
by John Paterson

The Bible Plan of Salvation
by Carl Williams

Note: All of these books and tracts plus a complete listing
of Pentecostal products can be ordered from:
Pentecostal Publishing House
8855 Dunn Road
Hazelwood, MO 63042
314-837-7304 Ext. 7
E-mail: pphsales@upci.org
Or visit: pentecostalpublishing.com